B

GW00363760

THE FIELD BOOK
OF HARDY GARDEN PLANTS

Also published

The Third Field Bedside Book, edited by Wilson Stephens

THE FIELD BOOK
OF HARDY GARDEN PLANTS

DEREK TILLEY

David & Charles: Newton Abbot

0 7153 5872 3

© THE FIELD, 1973

All rights reserved. No part of this
publication may be reproduced, stored
in a retrieval system, or transmitted,
in any form or by any means, electronic,
mechanical, photocopying, recording or
otherwise, without the prior permission
of David & Charles (Holdings) Limited

Set in eleven on thirteen point Plantin
and printed in Great Britain
by Latimer Trend & Company Ltd Plymouth
for David & Charles (Holdings) Limited
South Devon House Newton Abbot Devon

Contents

List of Illustrations

List of Illustrations

Introduction

Enthusiastic plantsmen can be accused of having their noses so buried in the soil that they rarely have time to sit back and survey the results of their efforts at leisure. At the opposite extreme the less enthusiastic gardener will want the maximum visual rewards for the least possible effort. For those of the latter persuasion there is unfortunately no easy way since a garden, being a living thing, will constantly need care and attention.

Initially there is no short cut to success but with intelligent planning and planting the garden should become an increasing source of enjoyment. The use of labour-saving ground cover and foliage plants over broad areas will go a long way to make a natural and trouble-free garden. Spreading shrubs and self-supporting tall perennials that need no staking will also furnish the ground and only require occasional maintenance and above all dispense with the annual digging over of large areas.

Once plants are comfortably established their well-being is not enhanced by constant digging or hoeing around their roots and the amount of hand weeding necessary should decrease as they spread to cover the soil. Plants should always be chosen to suit the soil and whether one gardens on clay, chalk, sand or peat there are always plants to suit the situation that will grow naturally however difficult the site or aspect.

Choice of Plants

The nature of a new garden in particular will change rapidly over the first years as trees and shrubs gain height and spread. Dappled shade can be one of the more important aspects in creating the right conditions for many favourite plants. The wide range of good decorative trees available gives scope for planting something of character and beauty rather than the ubiquitous cherry or laburnum, beautiful though they are. Dual purpose trees with seasons of flower and fruit or those with handsomely marked bark or variegated leaves should always be considered to extend colour and interest throughout the season.

Most gardeners relish the challenge of cultivating something new or mildly temperamental, and the scope for growing some of the less common and more interesting plants is increased as a garden matures. A few specialist nurseries dealing in uncommon but superb hardy perennials, alpines and shrubs supply the kind of plant that keeps a garden alive with curiosity and spurs the gardener on to growing plants with a wider range of form and interest.

Hardy plants with well shaped and handsomely marked leaves can make a permanent tapestry of green to cover the soil and keep the garden relatively weed free. Against such a background can be set self-reliant flowering plants such as astrantias, hardy fuchsias, peonies and roses, always remembering to choose plants with a natural grace that will sit easily in the whole setting.

The importance of having the garden well furnished through-out the whole year cannot be overstated. Even in midwinter there can be a few flowers to brighten the scene whether they be in the form of lowly aconites and hellebores, or the shrubby winter jasmines and autumn cherry which flowers intermittently in the winter during mild spells. Only by making full use of a selection of the immense range of plants available can one hope to get the full visual value from a garden.

One of the great virtues of gardens is their individuality. There is a wealth of plant material from many parts of the world, and in spite of the vagaries of the climate plants from many countries adapt and thrive in most parts, provided a little thought and care is given to their needs.

Some of the plants that are now grown and that are the very essence of gardening were not available a century ago, but with new collected plants coming on the market and the hybridists' improved offerings there is now a wide selection of good plants for all soils and purposes.

The plots of bedded half hardies and the herbaceous borders of pre-war days are now seldom seen. Expense and shortage of labour balanced against a relatively short season of beauty is the reason for their disappearance. Instead there are the mixed border and alpine and woodland gardens which allow for less colourful but more interesting plants with the accent on decorative leaves of all shapes and textures. There is a great vogue for plants with fine leaves such as hostas, euphorbias and bergenias, while the list of grey, silver and blue leaved plants make a valuable contribution to any planting scheme. With the inclusion of evergreens, shrubs and winter flowering hellebores and heathers, this type of border can look presentable and offer something of interest for twelve months of the year as well as providing a home for some of the choicer subjects.

On the premise that no garden is ever perfect, the planting season should not only be a time for finding places for new plants but an opportunity for modifying existing schemes and alteration of plant associations. In spring when the bulk of the border plants are beginning to make growth one should be able to stand back and take stock of the efforts of the previous months.

It would be a happy gardener indeed who could say that all his schemes and problems had been dealt with successfully. Knowing what modification is needed to improve a planting when everything is in full bloom and then carrying out the project when all growth has died back is a hazardous operation full of trial and error.

Even in gardens that have been established for only a few years, some plants will inevitably get out of hand and should be ruthlessly dealt with. Alarming things can happen even in the most carefully prepared sites. Pernicious weeds begin to show on what was imagined to be well cleared ground or a questing root from a clump of acanthus will wander far and wide to emerge from the centre of a choice but weaker plant. Shrubs which a few years ago had ample space between them will begin to crowd each other out. Too close planting of shrubs is a common fault, especially when first planting a garden. The desire to cover every square foot of earth is natural and has much to commend it but as plantings become too dense the less worthy plants must be taken out.

One of the basic rules which Victoria Sackville West applied to her great garden at Sissinghurst, in England, was never to retain for a second year that which displeased in the first. While all gardeners should experiment with new introductions and some of the less common species, unsuitable and unpleasing subjects should be rejected as soon as it is apparent that they are not the plant for your garden or one has no great liking for them.

There are so many good plants available to the gardener, and one cannot possibly grow them all, that it must be a matter of preference which one chooses. Over-reliance on the too easy plants that unfailingly give a mass of colour can be a basic mistake.

Introduction

Gardens that are a riot of mauve and white in spring with aubrietia and arabis or a solid mass of yellow and purple in late summer with heleniums and Michaelmas daisies, usually have little else to offer in interest for the remainder of the year.

※※※※※※※※※

Autumn Leaf Colour

When choosing ground-cover plants for the border it is not often realised that several of them can make a valuable contribution in the autumn by the brilliance of their turning leaves. Even the common strawberry can be transferred into a highly decorative and colourful rosette as the leaves turn to crimson and bronze. One of the best ground-cover plants of all is *Geranium macrorrhizum* with neat rounded leaves of intense green. In autumn these take on clean shades of crimson and vermilion and last in beauty until the first severe frosts finally put an end to the show. This plant will thrive in almost any soil or situation but seems to colour best in poor stony soils in full sun.

One other hardy geranium that will give a reliable autumn show is *G. punctatum*. The angular leaves of this plant are pale yellow in spring, and decorated with five maroon spots. During the summer the leaves are mid-green but in autumn they will often revert to yellow, a colour which contrasts strikingly with the five spots.

The large leaves of the various forms of bergenia can also make brilliant accents of colour. With these plants the individual leaves change to shades of scarlet and yellow and are all the more effective when seen against the fresh green of the young leaves. The varieties *B. purpurea*, *B. abendglut* and Ballawley hybrid have leaves which turn to a dull plum purple during the winter and are extremely effective when placed alongside silver-leaved plants.

Tellima grandiflora purpurea also has leaves which take on

13

tones of purple and bronze for the winter months. This plant has particularly fine rounded leaves, deeply veined and lobed. It is a plant for the part shade and is at its best as a foliage plant with Bowle's Golden Grass as a companion for the spring. The ordinary green form is also a good evergreen subject, the leaves of these becoming burnished with bronze and the veins deepening in colour. A plant which should be seen more often for its ruby red foliage is *Saxifraga fortunei*, Wadas variety. This is not evergreen but its intriguing leaves are colourful in season. Its habit of late flowering makes it especially valuable and in a mild autumn its crimson leaves are topped with showers of starry white flowers. In winter it is best given a light covering of leaves as protection against the worst of the frosts.

Roses are not often considered in the context of autumn leaf colour but the *rugosa* species and their forms have deeply veined leaves which become suffused with a soft butter yellow before they fall. The varieties Frau Dagmar Hastrup and Roseraie De L'Hay, two of the best in this group are particularly colourful in autumn.

Soil

There are few gardeners who would describe their soil as ideal and for those who garden on cold clays the dangers of autumn planting are manifold. The question of what can be safely planted or split up and replanted at the end of the year largely depends on one's soil and situation together with a knowledge of the type of plants one prefers to grow.

Less common, or rare plants that are of doubtful hardiness, are best planted in spring and in succeeding seasons need to be treated with some circumspection when dividing and replanting. Many of these, mainly introductions from abroad, will tolerate quite low temperatures but any hint of excessive moisture at the roots will quickly cause the plants to deteriorate and die.

In reasonably cultivated soils the roots of most plants are far safer left to their own devices through the winter instead of having to re-establish under adverse conditions. Most of the better gardening catalogues give definite indication of plants that should be reserved for spring planting, but when in doubt plant in spring, preferably when the first shoots are appearing and the plant is beginning to move.

If autumn planting must be carried out, raised beds are partly the answer in heavy soils especially if the top 12in or so are enriched and lightened with peat and coarse sand or weathered ashes. The problem is also partially solved when gardening on a hillside or terraced slopes with retaining walls that offer almost unlimited scope for winter protection and improved drainage.

In any garden there is obviously only a limited number of sheltered corners and these spots must be reserved for those plants and bulbs that will not stand extremely low temperatures.

On exposed heavy ground, good drainage is essential for healthy plants and while initial deep digging is necessary the condition of the top few inches of soil may make all the difference when growing such things as meconopsis and other plants with soft basal rosettes all of which are likely to rot at the collar in a wet season.

Grit in any form is a valuable addition to the surface of heavy soil. Besides draining moisture away from the most vulnerable parts of the plants it has a deterrent effect on the slugs and snails which do a great deal of damage to new shoots and young growth.

Some plants have an extremely brief dormant period, usually occurring at an awkward time for work in the borders. Peonies are a good example. Never the easiest plants to handle with their fleshy brittle roots, they only rest for a few weeks at the end of summer before the strong new buds of next year's growth begin to appear at the crown of the plant. By October or November they are well developed and are easily damaged when being dug up and replanted. For a good start initial planting of this type of plant is always better from pot grown material, preferably in early spring when conditions are improving.

One of the benefits of gardening on clay is that plants are rarely lifted out of the soil by hard frosts as so often happens on lighter soils. Even with the addition of generous helpings of grit, compost, peat or anything else that will improve its texture, clay remains a glutinous and stodgy mass that is best left alone in wet weather or presents a concrete-hard fissured surface after a few days' sun. For healthy plants good drainage is essential on clay.

The bulk of the top spit of soil will remain moist long after other soils have dried out and it is this quality that is so essential to many plants that will wilt at the slightest sign of drought. Astilbes, astrantias, phlox and *Anaphalis triplinervis* are all inclined to droop, and on lighter soils need daily watering in dry periods. Enthusiastic efforts to lighten clay can be overdone. Over-generous amounts of coarse sand and peat may result in failure with some plants that one could previously grow to perfection besides providing a scratching ground for every cat from miles around.

Surface rooting plants can be almost impossible in sandy soils; phlox and monarda in particular need a good moist stodge round their roots which rarely penetrate more than a few inches.

There are a surprising number of plants that insist on a good stiff loam or clay for their well-being and if this condition is not met little success can be expected. Some gardeners find acanthus difficult to establish on light and shallow soils, but once established in clay it will send its long fleshy roots through the most atrocious soil and spread sometimes too vigorously to mix with nearby plants.

The hardy bamboos which are becoming increasingly popular

for their decorative and evergreen qualities also prefer a moisture
retaining soil. Wet, ill-drained clays are not suitable but a clay
that has been enriched and mulched with humus will make a
perfect home for these elegant evergreens. As a contrast to the
narrow lance-shaped leaves of the bamboos, the broad heart-
shaped leaves of the hostas are a perfect foil. This is another
family of plants that look sad where the drainage is too fierce.
Together with lysimachias, ligularias and rodgersias they will
excel at the water's edge, but as few of us have water in the garden,
moist clay is the next best thing.

Like the hostas, so many of the plants mentioned have succulent
leaves and stems that are an open invitation to the slugs and
snails of all types that abound on clay soils. Unless kept under
control from early spring onwards they can be the cause of unsightly foliage for the remainder of the growing season.

While clay can never be the ideal medium, it is for many plants
preferable to lighter soils whose subsoil is often pure unsustaining
sand.

To many gardeners who have a high pH content in their soil
the sight of some well-grown lime-hating plant in another's
garden arouses regret if not outright envy. Imitation would be a
mistake however, since plants should always be selected to suit
the soil, especially trees and larger shrubs whose roots will
eventually become too expansive for any pit of prepared soil.
If this happens they will either die outright, or begin to show
symptoms of chlorosis and be a permanent rebuke to the gardener
and a misery to behold.

It should be possible however, for those who really wish to
grow some of the smaller and shallow rooted lime haters to do
so by preparing raised beds of suitable soil and then making quite
sure that any watering or liquid feeding is carried out with rainwater only and never with water from the tap. Since raised beds
with their sharp drainage may need frequent and thorough waterings in dry weather, the size of the beds should be limited as

most small gardens of today will only have room for one butt of rainwater.

Lime-hating alpines are comparatively easy, their very small-ness makes them suitable for troughs of peaty soil but a raised bed or retaining wall will be ideal for some of the slightly larger ground-cover plants such as *Gaultheria procumbens,* the creeping wintergreen. This delightful evergreen with pebbled leaves of different hues is a rapid carpeter in the right conditions and is most attractive in all seasons. The white flowers show up well against the leaves as do the scarlet berries which persist through the winter.

Among the ericaceous plants there are some which should be in all gardens if only because they give colour and effect at a time in the year when little else will. Good winter colour from Decem-ber to March can be had from heathers and fortunately most of the winter flowering kind will tolerate lime and should grow well provided they are planted firmly and with plenty of peat round the roots. A completely lime-free bed will allow some of the varieties with fine foliage to be grown. The colour and texture of the foliage of some species is as colourful as any flower and makes excellent all-year-round plants.

The shrubby trailer Lithospermum has definite dislikes about lime but can be successfully grown on a raised wall in humus with a sheet of plastic lining the ground underneath the eight or nine inches of peat. This is an excellent way to provide the right conditions for fussy plants but adequate drainage must be pro-vided otherwise the soil will become waterlogged and sour, another condition that this group of plants will not tolerate.

Frost Protection

The period over which many gardens are subject to frost is a long one with spells of varying cold from October to May. Frosts experienced before Christmas are in some areas of short duration and do little lasting or fatal damage to hardy plants. During these months too much protection is probably not a good thing. We still have occasional warm and sunny days when new growth should be discouraged and the previous summer's growth should be allowed to harden naturally.

The prolonged frost of January and February when the temperature does not rise above freezing point for days on end is an entirely different matter. Together with the biting winds that prevail in these weeks much damage can be done to young shrubs, especially evergreens. The loss of moisture through the leaves in newly planted evergreens is not matched by the water taken up by the unestablished roots and the plant quickly deteriorates.

Close protective screens or wrapping can prevent much of the moisture loss. Polythene sheeting does the job admirably, but shrubs shrouded in transparent or hideous green plastic sheets do not look particularly attractive. When manufacturers make garden plastics in less startling colours, they will almost certainly be more widely used. Surrounding circles of chicken wire supported by canes and loosely filled with leaves are much easier on the eye and provide first-class protection through which air can circulate. Beech leaves are good for this purpose since they dry out quickly after rain and are slow to settle down into a soggy mass. Mattresses of leaves, bracken or straw between chicken wire can serve a similar purpose for screening tender wall and climbing shrubs and generally have more stability than flimsy sheeting when large shrubs are to be sheltered.

Too often leaves are swept up and burned as soon as they fall. Collected and spread on borders and between shrubs they make valuable insulation and mulching material for the winter months and can be eventually composted. Generous layers of leaves used like this will prevent the soil from becoming deeply frosted or panned by heavy rains. Leaves removed from lawns can be used for this purpose and will partly break down by the following spring into valuable humus.

Most gardens should be able to provide enough natural material that can be utilised for the protection of the more tender plants. Herbaceous and border plants can also benefit by a mulch of leaves. As a last resort the gardener can be grateful for the first blanket of snow to protect his plants from the worst frosts and cutting winds.

Larger and more substantial dead leaves from border plants can also be used loosely to cover tender plants. Leaves that do not decay too quickly like ferns, some of the larger artemisias and tough fibrous leaves of iris or antholyza are all good and not too unsightly. The profuse top growth of *Clematis orientalis* can be draped over the tender buds of various types of hydrangea to give protection. Such material is ideal since it will break the worst effects of frost, but is open enough to allow a normal circulation of air.

Dead flower heads should be left on tender shrubby plants whenever possible and not removed until early spring. Not only will they give added protection to the next season's buds but they will also provide an element of decoration to the winter garden.

Severe frosts have a habit of partly lifting newly planted shrubs out of the ground and loosening the soil around the main stem. If this happens the soil should be trodden down firmly as soon as practicable before following winds and rain can do further damage to the plant.

Shrubs are more difficult to protect from the effects of snow and few gardens come through a winter without some damage in the form of broken branches or flattened plants.

Shapely and properly pruned shrubs are far less likely to suffer damage than those which have been allowed to become leggy and lax. Small shrubs like lavender, santolina and the hebes can be worst hit unless occasional cutting back and trimming has been carried out during the previous growing season, to keep the plants sturdy and compact.

In mild winters it is improbable that losses from autumn planted material will be heavy, but on badly drained clays some shrubs and trees take exception to an excess of water lying about their roots from the heavy rains of the first weeks of the year.

Spring Hazards

The main season of dashed hopes and bitter disappointment, however, usually comes with the dry cold winds and near drought condition of early spring. From the first day of spring we tend to expect too much from our gardens, and relax the precautions we have taken to protect our plants.

Newly planted conifers are notorious for their habit of surviving the winter months, only to succumb to the cutting winds of early spring. As with most, evergreen planting should be done either in September, early enough for the plant to make new roots before winter, or delayed until May when the roots and growing system become active again. If planting is done in the colder months new roots cannot form in time to take up and replace moisture that is continually being lost through the leaves.

The drying winds of March will soon put paid to the majority of such unestablished and insecure plants and the brown tell-tale signs of death, usually from the top downwards will soon be apparent.

Even when planting times are observed correctly and pot-grown plants are used to eliminate root disturbance the moisture loss is noticeable and daily care in the form of watering and spraying will be advisable on dry days until the plant is settled in.

Some evergreens, notably holly, will drop their leaves after replanting to prevent too much loss of water and so conserve their vigour in readiness for making new growth later in the summer.

The most convenient and probably the best method of protecting exposed young evergreens is to enclose them in a sleeve of hessian or polythene for the critical weeks. Unsightly as it is, this will do much to prevent the foliage drying out, leaving burnt-out ugly tips. A periodic soaking of the ground around the roots followed by a thick mulch of bracken or peat to prevent evaporation is also advisable under most early spring conditions.

The hardy bamboos which are mostly evergreen are becoming increasingly popular but are decidedly touchy about transplanting. This should never be attempted before the end of April but when established they will tolerate far dryer soils than was originally supposed.

The transplanting of any young shrub or tree is obviously a shock to its system and at least a year must be allowed for recovery and re-establishment. Some will resent disturbance more than others and sulk all through the spring and early summer months, so that the gardener is driven to distraction by their sad appearance. The Indian bean, *Catalpa bignonioides,* a late leafing tree at the best of times will often not show a leaf until August, after being planted the previous autumn.

If newly planted deciduous shrubs and trees are not showing signs of breaking into leaf at the appropriate time they should not be dug up and discarded out of hand. A fairly reliable test as to whether a plant is alive or not is gently to scrape the bark with a thumbnail. If the exposed area is green one can be satisfied that the plant is still alive and worth keeping in the ground. The shrubby potentillas are an exception to this rule. Even when alive and healthy the interior of their woody stems look dry and brown.

Most good catalogues will give the correct time for planting, and conscientious nurserymen will not deliver suspect plants until the danger period is past. Hardy border and herbaceous plants also have their quota of temperamentals that must be treated with consideration in the early stages. Agapanthus, fuchsias, phormiums and yuccas and many of the grey-leaved plants all benefit from spring planting no matter how hardy they are when established.

Tidying Up—or Not

The gardener should pause for consideration before wholesale cutting down and tidying up at the end of the growing season. Old stems afford many plants the protection they need from frost if they are to come through the winter unharmed. Plants like hydrangeas with dormant buds and others which start into growth early in the new year need this protection but there are many whose skeleton form is so good and resistant to the worst winter weather that they should be left standing at least until the early spring to provide winter decoration. Most astilbes are splendid in this role. The stems are tough and they and the flower heads turn a rich red brown which colours well in the winter sun. *Iris sibirica*, similarly upright, is also worth keeping.

Tall spiky outlines are especially valuable in the winter and teasels will remain immaculate. Odd clumps left standing at strategic points do much to add interest and they are superior to the thistles, which get untidy by mid autumn. It is tempting to try to keep eryngiums but these soon lose their neat appearance as the seeds fall.

On a smaller scale the easy and popular ice plants die off gracefully and last well. The variety *Sedum aizoon* colours best to a rich brown and the small, star-like flowers which dry to the same colour are especially attractive when rimed with frost. Hostas, on the other hand, make a messy exit and the dead leaves are best cleared away as soon as possible. The large blue leaved *H. siboldiana* is the only variety that one can rely on for good seedheads and these are excellent. Quickly fading to a delicate ivory colour, the jet-black seeds hang persistently from the open pods all winter although one always expects them to fall.

No claim could be made for beauty of the dead stems of bergamot, but these have a delicious fragrance which is released when brushed against; the plants should always be left standing if grown close to a path. The dead stems are also fragrant, if less powerfully, in many mints and, while of no decorative value, they are hardly unsightly.

If dead leaves of border plants are going to be good in winter they usually give every indication of their future intentions and should be left alone. The rich tobacco-brown leaves of *Geranium endressii* remain clean and fresh and make pleasing clumps. When caught by the sun the spreading mats of leaves of *Polygonum affine* have red and pink tints and are almost as showy as the summer display of flowers. The leaves of the taller *P. campanulatum* fall quickly but the knotted stems turn a rich carmine red. Since there is usually a mat of new deep green leaves at the base, this plant can be quite a feature.

Although one can have a surprising amount of colour in the garden from winter-flowering plants, these are mostly cool colours and the complimentary rich reds and browns are best supplied by the previous season's dead leaves.

Plant Names

Few gardeners are botanically minded enough to name all plants they grow in their gardens by their correct botanical names. There are those who are put off by having to deal with what at first sight can appear to be complicated jargon.

Of the thousands of species of plants available to the gardener only a small proportion have genuine common names that are universally known. Many people prefer the common names, most of which are beautiful as well as being imaginatively descriptive. How much more pleasant it is to be able to use evocative names like Wake Robin, Toad Lily, Cranesbill or Hounds Tongue instead of the botanical or latin forms that few people fully understand.

Some botanical generic names have become so familiar that they are now universally accepted and in common usage. Chrysanthemum, dahlia, fuchsia and camellia are a few that have been accepted as such, the last three being named after the plant collectors Dahl, Fuchs, and Kamell.

Of the older garden plants that have come back into favour over the last quarter of a century, there are many with delightful names to roll off the tongue, Pig Squeak, Lambs Tongue, Lady's Mantle and Cotton Lavender are all plants known well enough to merit description by these familiar epithets. Yet they are almost always referred to in gardening circles by the less easily remembered and sometimes tongue-twisting botanical names of *Bergenia cordifolia*, *Stachys lanata*, *Alchemilla mollis* and *Santolina chamaecyparissus*.

Difficulties encountered in the use of common names arise from variations between different localities. This applies particularly to garden forms of native plants, and for the not too sophisticated gardener it will be practically impossible to order a specific form of a plant from a modern catalogue without some elementary knowledge of nomenclature. The discerning gardener will need to be botanically correct and use the right classification of genera, species and cultivar in acquiring a particular plant.

Except for some of the species, there are few roses with complicated botanical names. As a favourite and popular flower most of the old ones have such beautiful and memorable names that it is almost worth growing them for these alone. Those with a French flavour are especially beautiful with their historical association. Names like Belle de Crecy, Cardinal de Richelieu, Duchesse de Montebello and Reine des Violettes are difficult to resist in such good and colourful garden plants. Only towards the end of the nineteenth century do we find a hint of coarseness creeping into these names as in that small bourbon rose of 1894 with the superlative title of Champion of the World. A glance through a list of modern roses while listing many attractive names will confirm a deplorable tendency towards the brash and sentimental with Colour Wonder, Flaming Sunset and Orange Sensation.

Odorous Plants

Some plants suffer unduly from the unkind and sometimes un-deserved descriptive names by which they are commonly known. Often they are names which were acquired in the dim past when the plants were grown for medicinal purposes, and their less attractive qualities emerged only with processing. The smell of the common valerian grown as a garden flower is inoffensive enough but when the roots are dried the resulting odour is most unpleasant and only appreciated by cats and their arch-enemy, the rat. Indeed until the end of the last century dried valerian root was much used as a bait for rat traps.

One of the noblest of all winter flowering plants, *Helleborus foetidus*, which is almost universally admired for its well cut dark green leaves and bunches of livid green flowers, is viewed with suspicion when called by its common name of stinking hellebore. In fact the odour is unnoticeable unless sought after and since this is a plant for shady corners and back-of-the-border positions and flowering in the winter months, only the most delicate and sensitive noses could be offended.

Saddled with the same unfortunate epithet *Iris foetidissima* can at worst be accused of smelling of roast beef when the leaves are bruised. Although the flowers of this plant are relatively insignificant the beautiful evergreen leaves and long lasting seedpods, split to show rows of orange berries, make it a worthwhile foliage plant for winter.

Other plants without such warnings in their names can be decidedly unpleasant and should be avoided at all costs unless one is a collector of unusual plants. Fortunately the real offenders are few, the most obvious example being *Dracunculas vulgaris*, a striking plant in leaf and flower but with an odour so strong that it needs a position well away from the house or well used paths. There are many gardeners who prefer not to grow any of the decorative onion family. While their typically garlic smell is undoubtedly present, it should prove innoxious if planted a little way from the path's edge where it will not be brushed against.

Such odours will always be a matter of personal taste. Even geraniums and chrysanthemums are despised by some who find their strong but not unpleasant smelling foliage a little too much. The astringent smell of the Vatican Sage or the musty odour of rue will also rouse inexplicable passions but it is plants with the downright rank and unpleasant odours of cats or drains that one should guard against. Such plants exist and while nurserymen are naturally reluctant to list the faults of specific plants there is always the danger that one will unknowingly be landed with a shocker. Always beware of the catalogue description that describes the fragrance of a plant as interesting or curious. Some of the dogwoods can give a nasty shock when one unwittingly inhales deeply from a bunch of their small flowers and the attractive pyracantha flowers which resemble the hawthorn are little better on close contact. Fortunately most of these scents are close and only carry under exceptional conditions but if they are otherwise good garden plants one can usually mask this fault by planting more sweetly scented flowers nearby.

1

Foliage

No matter how much we admire flowers of one kind or another the decorative importance of leaves is paramount in the well-furnished garden. There are gardeners who choose plants for their leaves alone, regarding flowers as a dividend. If a garden is to look presentable the whole year through, this is not a bad principle.

When one considers the wide range of leaf colour, shape and texture with which the gardener can work, this attitude to planting has unlimited possibilities. It would be impossible to describe in words the number and variety of greens found in a reasonably planted garden; they range from the soft yellow greens of Lady's Mantle to the deepest greens of hellebore and yew. The delicacy of hue of even the strongest greens allows them to be planted alongside each other with contrast and perfect clarity and providing the leaf shape has strength and character the garden will also be strong in design. There are few sights more irritating in a garden than that of masses of blowsy unexciting leaves produced

28

by overplanting such things as Michaelmas daisies or phlox. Stems of plants like this can, with a little imagination, be masked by more worthwhile foliage and the use of grey or silver leaves is one of the best ways of breaking up and cooling great masses of green.

Colour in Foliage

The cult of the grey and silver plant has grown enormously in recent years. Good blue foliage is more difficult to come by but the few plants that are generally available are excellent and their leaves can be described as blue not greenish-blue. The small shrub *Ruta graveolens*, Jackman's Blue, is an easy and attractive plant and not seen as often as these qualities would merit. The blue filigree foliage is good for at least ten months of the year and its only requirement is drastic cutting back in the early spring. The ample heart-shaped foliage of *Mertensia pterocarpa* is a beautiful translucent blue and hung with arching sprays of blue flowers. The large-leaved hostas and prostrate aceanas both have varieties with blue leaves and these are never seen to better advantage than when contrasted with golden foliage.

There are a surprising number of plants that have golden leaved forms or golden variegations. These are particularly useful for contrast and lighting up dark corners—the kind of conditions in which they thrive. In full sun many of them burn and become browned at the edges. The best of these have the whole leaf suffused with yellow like Mr Bowle's Golden Grass; the golden meadowsweet or the golden form of *Lamium maculatum* should be sought in preference to the more spotty variegations.

The strongest leaf colour of all is provided by the purple- and bronze-leaved plants. These should not be overworked or the result may be heavy and depressing, though few of them have leaves the whole year through. Most reliable of all are the carpeting bugles and aceanas, the former with robust shining leaves of purple or bronze that are always the picture of health. Apart from the purple-leaved sage which is decidedly scruffy during the winter months, gardeners would be wiser to rely on the purple-leaved deciduous shrubs and trees. The purple plum and nut and the copper beech can be supplemented with the various coloured forms of *Cotinus coggygria* which range from wine red to purple.

Grey Leaves and Stems

Grey-leaved plants are among the most useful of all foliage plants. Their one failing is the miserable appearance they assume in wet weather but they can quickly regain their good looks after rain. All parts of *Stachys lanata* are thickly clothed with white downy hairs. This plant will send up candelabras of fleecy spikes with small mauve hooded flowers but in excessive rain leaves and stems become saturated and the result is a tangled mass of sodden grey. Only in tolerably dry weather does the foliage which is so important to such plants remain clean and white.

Furry foliage can be very beautiful in any sunny situation and there are subjects of all sizes and shapes from the lowly rosettes of the hawkweed, *Hieraceum villosum*, to the towering spikes of *Verbascum bombyciferum*. All that is needed is sun and a soil that is not too rich and with adequate drainage.

The verbascum which can rise to 10ft or more is a most imposing plant with a stem thickly clothed with white down and studded for much of its length with lemon yellow flowers. Effective ground cover is made by the white basal leaves in the form of huge rosettes which are attractive in winter and become whiter as the spring weather improves. Few plants of this height will stand upright without some support but stakes are rarely needed for this biennial which once introduced into the garden will seed itself generously.

For the front of a sunny border the hawkweeds will again do best in a fairly poor soil. This a plant with fine foliage and rather poor daisy-like flowers. These are best removed so that the full beauty of the leafy rosettes is not marred.

Some of the poppies have good rosettes of soft hairy leaves that are as striking as any flower. One of the best is *Meconopsis regia* whose leaves have a sheen of silver and gold and is a most valuable subject for a winter planting. For full beauty of winter foliage the leaves should be protected in very wet spells by a pane of glass supported by wire or an open sided cloche. Failing that it is sometimes possible to position the plant in a vertical crevice of a wall. In this way most of the rain will drain off and the crowns will not rot. This is a common failing with plants of this type and the woolly leaved sage, *Salvia argentea*, should be grown in this way whenever possible. This is another plant that is usually grown for its foliage effect only, although the 3ft spikes of ivory flowers are quite pleasant and a useful height for many positions.

Some of the most interesting flowers of all the greys are those of the various forms of the easily grown anaphalis. The best and most easily controlled form of all is the tufted *A. triplinervis*. This plant makes a 12in dome of handsome grey leaves which is eventually surmounted by wide heads of pearl coloured everlasting flowers. This is one of the few grey plants that will not tolerate drought and seems to do best in a fairly heavy soil. Unlike other greys, it will also thrive in partial shade or under a north wall. The flowers last in beauty for an incredibly long time and are well worth keeping on well into the winter. Although they do not take kindly to rain and excessive moisture, they quickly regain their shape at the first sign of sun and drier conditions.

Anaphalis margaritacea has the same kind of wide branching heads of wiry flowers with yellow centres but can be a nuisance in some positions as it spreads by underground stolons and will run even in the stiffest soils. The tiny silver shoots are irresistible when they push through the ground very early in the year and at this stage it is wise to remove any unwanted stems if the plant has spread out of bounds. The roots rarely lie more than a few inches below the surface of the soil and are easily traced back to the point of growth for removal. In habit this plant is completely different from *A. triplinervis*. From the first tiny shoots a forest of erect 12in stems arise with rather flatter and less fluffy heads of flowers that could individually be mistaken for helichrysums.

Similar but smaller in all parts, *A. nubigena* can be a useful addition to the rock garden although it is rather difficult to come across these days. The largest member of the family is *A. yedoensis*, another erect plant growing to some 20in in height. This particular plant needs careful twigging early in the growing season as the weight of the fluffy heads of flowers when wet is usually too great for the slender stems to support. The long lasting qualities and lightness of appearance of all forms of anaphalis make them indispensable plants for sunny situations where they will provide good ground cover and interest for months.

The artemisias are probably the hardiest and most useful family of all the greys for garden work, for as ground cover and underplanting to roses they are unsurpassed. The clean neutral greys and silvers of their leaves provide an excellent foil to brightly coloured blooms and strong coloured foliage.

One of the finest plantings in the famous White Garden at Sissinghurst, England, consists of a stretch of various artemisias interplanted, with white flowered border plants and the white *Lilium regale*. These together with white roses tower above a sea of grey and provide the shade and cool conditions necessary for the lilies.

Page 33 1 Astilbe arendsii Deutschland. *The astilbes are excellent plants for moist ground with well cut foliage and colourful blooms*

2 *The Crown Imperial,* Fritillaria imperialis, *an old garden plant and one of the most handsome in the spring border*

Page 34   3 *The foliage of the Meadowsweet,* Filipendula ulmaria aurea, *and of the glaucous* Hosta *Buckshaw Blue are at their best in a cool spot*
4 *The arrow-shaped leaves of* Arum italicum pictum *are marbled with cream and appear above ground in the autumn*

Two substantial artemisias, *A. absinthium* and *A. arborescens*, have a height of 2 or 3ft and are ideal between shrub roses. The former has an outstanding cultivar known as Lambrook Silver raised by Margery Fish, while the latter has attractive filigree leaves and is the most aristocratic grey of all.

Of the herbaceous kinds in this size range *A. ludoviciana* is almost white, flowers well, and spreads moderately by underground stolons. Since these stay near the surface they are rarely a menace to adjoining plants. The cultivar *A.* Silver Queen has fine elegantly cut leaves, but unfortunately it also has stems that are too weak to support its fine foliage and flower heads. Unless supported between shrubs or roses it tends to lie about in a most untidy manner and without such supports is best grown sprawling over a bank or low wall. The lower growing *A. pontica* with individual stems like pewter-coloured cypresses is a useful foliage plant when contrasted with the more solid leaves of such things as bergenias and sedums. This plant develops such a thick root mass that few weeds are likely to find a home between its stems.

The flowers of all the artemisias are insignificant but do not detract from the beauty of the plant. In some varieties notably *A. absinthium* a mild crop of seedlings result when the flower heads are left on. These are useful replacements since like sages and other fast growing shrubs they tend to become woody and unshapely after a few years and are best grubbed out and replaced with fresh young plants.

Most grey-leaved plants, the artemisias particularly, revel in hot sunbaked positions and given the maximum amount of light and sun will repay this kindness by producing lighter and cleaner foliage. If these conditions can be arranged together with a suitably contrasting background the foliage alone is worth a fairly important position. Some varieties are old cottage garden plants with old cottage names and association. They seem to be very much at home and looking their best against mellow brick or weathered stone. With names like Southernwood, Lad's Love,

Old Woman and Old Warrior, and their astringent aromatic qualities it is hardly surprising that they have retained their popularity and are being recognised as trouble-free plants for the modern garden.

Hostas

When using plain green leaves, boldness of form is essential. There is a huge range to choose from that will give the necessary contrast of shape and colour to keep the garden interesting throughout the growing season.

In all but the driest soils the hostas are some of the most adaptable plants of all. Natives of Japan, the nomenclature of the species and cultivars has for many years been somewhat confused and the only sure way to get the plant required was to see it growing in the nursery, but since they are such splendid and worthwhile plants time spent like this is never wasted.

For ground cover in light shade there is no better plant since it is in these conditions that clumps thrive and increase and, especially the glaucous varieties, produce the larger and better coloured leaves. They are, however, most accommodating plants and will grow in the extremes of shade and sun. The trumpet-shaped flowers rising in spikes above the leaves are borne freely when planted in sun although the leaves are usually smaller and the whole plant more compact. Plants grown in sunny positions need copious waterings in dry periods if the full glory of the plant is to be maintained. Conversely plants growing in shade or under a north wall produce magnificent leaves but fewer flowers. Providing enough moisture is available, they are not fussy about soil; and although originating in Japan will grow surprisingly well on chalky soils if humus is incorporated in the soil and mulchings of manure or compost are given at the beginning of the growing season. It is also advisable at this time to apply a slug killer round the crowns. Slugs and snails are the hostas' main enemy, attacking the leaves while still in the folded spiky stage. If this happens the beauty of the plant is ruined for the whole season, although it is possible to remove some of the outer leaves which are usually the worst affected.

In any soil they make sizeable clumps which increase slowly and as the roots make a solid and clawlike mass division is easily effected with a sharp spade or knife.

The flowers of all varieties are either white, mauve or pale lilac, held in sprays on tall stems well above the leaves. The dead stalks and seed heads are very persistent and will decorate the bare winter garden until cut down in the spring. Although the flowers are welcome in summer it is for the broad and showy leaves that most gardeners adore this plant. They are at their best in late spring and early summer when the colour variations are brightest. According to the varieties, there are plain or glaucous greens, cream and white variegations and two-toned greens. A recent introduction *H. tokudama variegata* has a glaucous green background flushed with primrose yellow. Like many rare and treasured plants it does not increase as quickly as its commoner relatives, although it is said to be just as hardy. Another newcomer is *H.* Yellow Edge. This plant has rather large grey-green leaves surrounded by a brilliant yellow margin and makes a most effective spot plant.

One nursery offers a selected variety of *H. sieboldiana* named Buckshaw Blue which has thick textured leaves of a very glaucous blue. With its dwarf and compact habit this could be a valuable plant especially in the smaller garden. That remarkable foliage plant *Hosta fortunei albo picta* has yellow leaves that are in the early months irregularly margined with shades of green. This is one of the most beautiful of all variegated plants in its early stages but as the season progresses the variegation disappears and the whole plant is suffused by a soft green.

Foliage

Most hosta leaves are broad, heart-shaped and prominently ribbed but there are other interesting shapes in the form of narrow leaved forms as well as varieties with undulating and wavy edges in both green and variegated forms. With these good garden qualities the plantain lilies are indispensable to all who value bold foliage, whether it be for decoration or ground cover. Hostas do the job admirably.

Green Ground Cover

Easy and even-tempered foliage plants that are indispensable to a good garden are so often taken for granted and do not receive the appreciation they deserve. This is particularly true of plants in one's own garden that unfailingly appear above soil each spring and perform their summer stint with little or no attention. Only when seen from a fresh viewpoint, usually in another's garden do we realise what excellent plants they are and the variety of possibilities they offer regarding design and individual use. The tough, easy-going but extremely beautiful Lady's Mantle is a case in point. This plant has few vices except occasional over-seeding and seems to be immune to pests and diseases. As with many seedlings the leaves of the young plants are most attractive and will lodge in any available crevice where their roots will delve between stones and eventually make large plants. The downy light green leaves of the best known form, *Alchemilla mollis,* have a particularly softening effect and associate well with old brick and most local stone. With their tendency to produce more seedlings than one can normally cope with they are one of the best plants for growing between the crevices of flagstones and will find all the nourishment they require through their tough stringy roots. This plant will in fact grow in any soil or situation and put up with the most appalling neglect. Only when it is planted in wet positions where its leaves are splashed with mud does it begin to look untidy, but it by no means resents the moisture. Never are they seen to better advantage than after an early summer shower when glistening raindrops are held in the rounded leaves, covered with minute silky hairs. At this time the generous display of feathery yellow stars on stiff wiry stems transform the plant into a frothy mound of delicate yellow-green. It is a splendid companion to purple- or blue-leaved plants. The solidity of the purple sages or the compact density of blue rue give an added contrast that can hardly be bettered in plant associations.

Tidy gardeners will remove the flower heads before the seeds ripen, but it is not often realised that if picked just before their peak they dry and keep their colour admirably for winter decoration. For anyone who wishes to cover a large area with good foliage at little cost there are a few plants with the exception of *Geranium macrorrhizum*, that will be equal to the task. Small plants 2ft or so apart will quickly increase in size, colonising the ground and producing enough seedlings to fill the intervening spaces. For such uses this alchemilla does not seem to resent cramped quarters and within a comparatively short time thickens up to become completely weed proof. Any gardener who has dug up an established clump will know what a dense ball of matted roots this plant makes. There are few weeds strong enough to find a home amid such a tangle.

Variegated Foliage

The better known *A. alpina* for rock gardens and walls is a delightful mat-forming plant, with exquisite divided deep green leaves finely edged with silver. This edging is an overlap of fine satiny hairs which completely coats the reverse side of the leaves.

39

If only the undersides were more readily visible this could be one of the finest dwarf foliage plants in the garden. The flowers of this dwarf variety are less important than the leaves and appear as pale green sprays of stars. Some gardeners remove these at an early stage to retain the neat rosettes which make such a splendid foil to more colourful alpines.

Many of the more interesting and choice variegated plants show their best colouring and markings from mid spring to early summer. A variegated astrantia *A. major variegata*, which is still rare and accordingly rather expensive, gives full value from its foliage from the time that the first brightly splashed leaves appear until they are eventually cut back by the first frost of autumn. This rarity can be grown as easily as the ordinary green-leaved form although it does not increase so rapidly or make such dense and robust clumps. The deeply divided leaves have bold markings of white and cream which are at their best when given a position in the sun and in a soil that remains fairly moist.

Requiring a similar moist situation although capable of putting up a better show in some shade, the variegated form of *Brunnera macrophylla* is another uncommon but fairly easy plant. In May and June while the leaves are developing the plant is decorated with long sprays of bright blue forget-me-not flowers. This is a rather sparse plant compared with the non-variegated type but the sage green leaves are so boldly margined with broad bands of cream that they make up in spectacle what they lack in substance. This brunnera is a tricky plant to move or divide since damage to the roots will almost certainly result in some of the leaves reverting to green.

One of the most striking of all variegated plants, grown for its foliage alone and now being listed in a few of the choicer catalogues is *Tovara virginiana variegata*. In the best forms the ovate leaves are boldly marked with a russet brown V, the light green background being suffused with patterns of cream and pink. There is nothing washy about the colours of this plant and by late summer it will have grown into a fine leafy clump some 2ft high and across. This plant is worthy of good soil and a position in light shade where it can remain without disturbance. It is an herbaceous plant and new shoots do not appear until late spring. Some protection in very exposed positions is advisable, preferably the backing of a hedge or wall.

The variegated form of *Iris pseudacorus* which initially has boldly striped leaves has the distressing habit of turning wholly green in late summer but is such a magnificent plant that it deserves a place in any border.

Grasses

One of the annual chores that should never be neglected in the border is that of keeping in bounds over-enthusiastic clumps of Ribbon Grass, or Gardeners Garters as it is more often called. This variegated grass with broad white stripes and graceful drooping leaves is most valuable when a light note is required but its invasive nature can be rather trying especially when its questing roots throw up clumps in the centre of a more valuable plant. Some gardeners clip it to a few inches above ground to give a carpet of fresh variegation but by doing this the characteristic drooping habit is lost.

Surprisingly many of the smaller hardy grasses which are so versatile as ground cover or edging plants are received with indifference or suspicion by many gardeners. There are now many varieties to choose from in a whole range of colours and variegation and almost all of these are easy plants suitable for most soils. Many of them have graceful outlines and look good as single plants, but used in mass or set in groups of five or seven they can also make splendid evergreen ground cover. Not everyone has a patch of rough grass in which to grow spring bulbs as they should be grown, but clumps of these smaller grasses will provide protection for the small bulbs and go some way to disguising their unsightly dying leaves after flowering.

One of the better grasses for this purpose is *Millium effusum aureum*, Mr Bowle's Golden Grass, with its young leaves of an almost luminous gamboge yellow. This is a grass that is best grown in a semi-shaded position where it will seed itself mildly but never become a nuisance.

Another golden grass with more permanent leaves is *Carex stricta aurea*. This grass makes extremely neat, stiff, 1ft high clumps and does best if given some shade and a fairly rich soil.

A fascinating small bulbous grass, with green and white variegations and bearing the formidable name of *Arrhenatherum elatius bulbosum variegatum*, is useful for small areas as it does not spread unduly although the bulbs multiply fast one above the other rather like antholyza.

For moist ground a grass that needs plenty of room is *Glyceria aquatica variegata*. This has stripes of yellow and sports grassy flower-spikes 2ft high. In drier soils it is less exuberant and for its full beauty is best as a waterside plant.

If a carpet is required a more satisfactory grass is the dwarf *Holcus mollis variegatus* which spreads by stolons and is only a few inches high. This is a good plant for growing between paving stones where it potters along happily and like the Ribbon Grass can be given an occasional crew-cut to keep the foliage fresh.

The most prized of all variegated grasses is the dainty clump forming *Molinia caerulea variegata* which flowers profusely on arching wiry stems. The flowers are some of the most attractive of all grasses with hints of violet blue in the anthers. This moorland grass increases very slowly and although some catalogues specify a lime-free soil it is not too fastidious and will tolerate some chalk.

Much of the value of these small grasses lie in their colour and

Foliage

variegations. There are few green grasses that are grown for their leaves alone but the range of golds, greys and bronze shades gives the gardener wide scope for their use, and there is nothing more useful in the natural garden for linking plantings or toning down the bright patches of colour.

For grey and silver, the festucas come into their own. The easiest and most striking being *F. ovina glauca*. This is a good all-the-year-round grass and has extremely neat flower heads. Even neater but definitely requiring sun and good drainage, *F. amethystina* is a rather choice plant of steel grey that is worth a special position in the rock garden. Most of these grasses are easily increased by division but attempts to propagate festucas from minute pieces almost certainly ends in failure and large clumps should not be divided into more than three or four pieces.

Bronze-coloured leaves are few among the grasses but the carex family contains two which are good garden plants. The largest, *C. buchananii*, a neat New Zealand sedge, has narrow copper-coloured leaves which spiral towards the tips. The smaller edition, *C. petriei*, is extremely deep in colour and in certain lights the leaves appear to be black. Both of these sedges need a peaty soil which retains some moisture.

Two giants among the grasses are *Miscanthus sinensis variegatis* and *M. sinensis zebrinus*, the former with leaves striped lengthwise with white and the latter having leaves banded crosswise with yellow. Both these grasses are gracefully erect and non-running. They are ideal as a foil for other plants or as windbreaks and providers of shade. Of these two *M. zebrinus* is the most free to flower but as with most plants grown for foliage, flowers are not of primary importance.

It is not generally realised that a considerable number of bamboos are perfectly hardy in our climate and if properly planted and sited, they can be the greenest foliage plants in the winter garden. The main requirements for good growth is moist soil and shelter from excessive wind although good sized established clumps of the taller kinds will make decorative and effective windbreaks, giving all year round protection.

Some bamboos tend to spread rapidly by underground stolons but these are not too difficult to contain if sliced round periodically with a sharp spade. The more rampant and vigorous kinds are obviously best left to those with large gardens and if allowed plenty of space can make most imposing groups when erect and arching varieties are contrasted. An effective method of keeping the more boisterous forms within bounds is to dig a ditch or trench round the clump and so confine the creeping rootstocks.

Plants growing in the wild usually attain much greater height than in our gardens but even so 15–20ft plants are not rare in Britain.

Garden bamboos are selected and grown for their leaves and stems, both of which have character and variation of size and colour ranging from dwarfs of 3ft to giants of 20ft or more. The flowering habits of the bamboos are curious, many being monocarpic and dying after flowering; the time taken to mature can be ten, fifty or even a hundred years or more. It is recorded in the RHS dictionary of gardening that *Sasa tessellata*, which was introduced into Britain in 1845, has not yet flowered. When flowering does occur, especially in species which flower on all stems, the whole plant dies. In many of these species all plants die simultaneously over a wide area, some being wiped out from whole countries. This is particularly true of plants in nature but while garden plants also die, the result is not so simultaneous. Introduction of new stock can then only be effected by seed which is presumably what happens with plants growing in their natural habitat.

Fortunately not all bamboos have such an abrupt ending, those which flower on some stems have others to carry on but with such longevity the eventual loss of a plant is of little concern.

2

Spring

In early spring when gardeners are waiting for the first full flush of bloom in the border, a few early flowering and perhaps less commonly grown subjects give interest and sharpen the appetite for things to come. It is surprising how many easy plants there are that one can grow but are seldom seen in gardens, their place being taken by far more troublesome bedding plants and uncertain novelties.

Epimediums are not grown nearly enough and with their delicate hanging flowers in various colours on wiry stems are at their best in early spring. Their divided, pointed and marbled leaves give perfect ground cover and ask only for a cool root run and some shade. Other than an annual dusting of bonemeal and the removal of old leaves, they require little attention and will thrive in most unpromising spots.

For a touch of summer in early spring *Waldsteinia ternata* will always oblige. This dwarf trailing plant with dense lobed foliage displays a mass of rich yellow strawberry-like flowers in

45

early spring, and for the rest of the year provides a shaggy mat of green no more than 3in high through which dwarf bulbs can be grown to extend the flowering season.

One of the prettiest trouble-free plants for this season is *Orobus vernus*, a member of the pea family. This is a small herbaceous type of plant about a foot high with numerous wiry stems growing from a central crown. The typical pea flowers are small but with their range of purple, blue, green and red veining the effect is that of shining amethysts.

Rhubarb

The leaves of various ornamental rhubarbs are exciting from the moment they begin to make growth. They shoot up at a prodigous rate which exceeds all expectation. Good feeding is obviously needed to produce such robust plants but they are not at all choosy about soil, providing it does not dry out. As waterside plants they are superb and in such a position are more likely to be allowed the space they deserve to show their fine leaves to advantage. The red-leaved cultivars are particularly worthy of careful siting and for full effect should be placed so that the leaves can be seen against a low morning or evening light. With the sunlight shining through them these take on attractive ruby tones patterned by the dark ribs on the undersides of the leaves. The best red-leaved form is *Rheum palmatum*, Bowle's variety. This is a fairly compact plant and not quite so large as some forms, fitting well into the smaller garden. In early summer the 6ft flowering stems bear panicles of bead-like crimson flowers and make one of the most imposing sights in the garden.

The green-leaved forms are no less decorative and are good for the larger scene having a variety of leaf shape. A curious and unusual 3ft high form is *R. alexandrae* with papery yellow bracts running the length of the flowering stem. This one can be more difficult to establish, but once settled down it can make a most attractive plant, quite unlike anything else in the garden.

Useful Early Spring Plants

Most forms of bergenia contribute superb colour to these leafless weeks. The hairy-leaved *B. ciliata* although not hardy is always one of the earliest to flower. Its pale green flowers usually begin to open in late March but if given a little overnight protection in the form of a cloche it should come to no harm.

The hardy *B. cordifolia* and *B. crassifolia* send up stout crimson stems topped with clusters of brilliant pink flowers above fresh green spoon-shaped leaves. The flowers are held well above the bold foliage and put on a bold and vigorous show. A number of new varieties have become available in recent years and all are good garden plants with the same huge leaves that are perfect ground cover.

For early colour of a different kind, the blues and dusky pinks of the lungworts and borages are indispensable. Some of the members of the borage family can be rather too generous with their seedlings, but in April their clean blue flowers are an asset to any garden and indispensable in shady spots. Such a plant is *Brunnera macrophylla,* a perennial with clean heart-shaped leaves and sprays of pure blue flowers. This plant never looks better than when growing in half shade or woodland conditions. In the border its place is at the back row where its leaves will make handsome ground cover after flowering. There is also a good variegated form with startling white markings.

47

The much smaller Blue-eyed Mary, *Omphalodes verna*, does not seed but increases by creeping stems and is an extremely neat plant for a shady corner. With similar bright blue flowers and well shaped leaves a slightly larger version, *O. cappadocica*, is said to be a more compact plant with rather better leaves. The aristocrat of the early borages is undoubtedly the mertensia and all its forms are commendable. The foliage of *M. virginica* lacks the coarseness of the other borages and has a soft glaucous sheen. The mauve-blue flowers hang gracefully from 2ft stems and when grown in moist rich soil it is one of the most beautiful of all spring plants. Two lesser known species, *M. ciliata* and *M. sibirica*, are also good plants, the latter having soft pink young flowers that become purple and blue in maturity. A newcomer, *M. pterocarpa*, Blue Drop, is described as having ample glaucous foliage and arching sprays of blue flowers which lasts for many weeks.

The coarse symphytums seed heavily and are best in the wild garden in groups where they will fend for themselves. They do however make fine winter rosettes of glabrous leaves and are good ground cover. The flowers, formed in terminal trusses, come in all colours and while not blatantly showy are curiously attractive. The best blue form is *S. peregrinum*, a tall species whose multi-branched stem reaches 4ft. The finest of all symphytums, if one can find it, is the variegated *S. uplandicum variegatum*, one of the most striking border plants and good in leaf for a long period.

The pulmonarias, begin to flower in late winter but they are at their best in the early weeks of April. These are good dual purpose plants with highly decorative leaves that improve in size and colour as the season progresses. The one with boldly spotted leaves that is normally grown is *Pulmonaria saccharata* and there are varying forms of this plant with extra large or distinctive spots. One form is so heavily marbled that practically the whole leaf is a silvery white; it is most effective when grown in half shade. Some gardeners would describe the leaves as coarse but the best forms have such good markings that they are well worth a place near the front of the border.

The green flowers of the spurges are not to everyone's liking, but they are deservedly gaining popularity and having once grown them few gardeners would be willing to do without. The various forms have widely differing habits from the low sprawling *E. myrsinites* to the towering croziers of *E. wulfenii* with intermediate sizes that will fit into most situations. Almost all hardy spurges are accommodating plants that will grow in the poorest of soil providing the situation is open and reasonably sunny. Most hardy forms have splendid evergreen foliage. In spring the flowers unfailingly open and may last in beauty for many weeks.

For woodland soils and shade the graceful *Uvularia grandiflora* from America is worth considering. This small plant throws up a mass of slender stems and soft green foliage. Although not often grown this is a useful plant to put between shrubs where the pale yellow flowers, which are rather like dog's tooth violets, make a substantial patch of colour.

In moist soil the marsh marigold, *Caltha palustris,* can be the highlight of the early spring garden. The double form is definitely superior to the single. The orange flowers have the typical buttercup sheen and stand out splendidly above the glossy rounded foliage.

A little later the taller and more showy buttercups put on a dazzling display. The globe flower, *Trollius x hybridus,* is usually the first to make an appearance and in moist soil makes a hefty 2ft clump covered with burnished golden flowers.

The cultivars of this species have a good colour range from pale yellow to shiny bronze, and are particularly effective when under-planted with brunnera or forget-me-nots which flower at the same time.

The single canary yellow *R. gouanii* has a long season and is one of the most graceful of all. The flowers are borne on long

49

slim stems that emerge from rosettes of grey-green leaves, clothed with silken hairs. This tuberous plant will spread moderately but rarely gets out of hand. The best double is *R. speciosus floreplena,* a bulbous species whose leaves can be mistaken for the common field buttercup in their early stages. When fully grown it is however a large and handsome plant with an interesting green sheen to its yellow petals.

The first flowers of the most untypical member of the buttercup family, the columbine, also appear in spring. Although charges of overseeding and indiscriminate hybridising can be levelled against it, the old fashioned Granny's Bonnet forms remain great favourites. The young leaves of the seedlings are extremely attractive and when thinning out there is a great temptation to leave small plants that would otherwise be discarded in a less attractive genus.

The various columbines have the widest colour range of all the buttercup family and the clusters of bird-like flowers swaying at the end of wiry stems make this one of the most graceful additions to the garden.

Nettles

Nettles come into flower very early but, as garden plants, they suffer from the reputation of the less attractive and painful wild species. Garden forms of wild plants are often far less robust when in cultivation, but this is not true of the lamiums which are tough, persistent and sometimes only too easy to grow. Indeed the variegated form of the Yellow Archangel, *Lamium galeobdolon variegatum,* has to be continually curbed unless given ample space to spread; but it is such a beautiful plant that it is worth this small chore. It is particularly useful in a dark and neglected corner where little else will grow or at the base of a hedge where

Page 51   5 *The double peonies like Bridal Veil rival the old roses for*
sheer flamboyance
6 *The beautiful single yellow* P. mlokosewitschii *blooms in April, and*
has a splendid tinted foliage for the rest of the season

Page 52   7 *Astrantias have intricately beautiful flowers, consisting of a cushion of florets surrounded by a collar of showy bracts*
8 *The green flowered* Bupleurum angulosum, *an intriguing plant for part shade. Waxy petals surround a boss of prominent stamens*

it will climb into the lower branches and then let droop its long trails of shining silvery leaves.

For rough areas, especially slopes in shady inhospitable places, there is no better ground-cover plant. The rapid spread is achieved by long whippy runners which radiate from the parent plant, rooting as they go at each leaf axil. The startling evergreen leaves are generously splashed with silver and indigo and are at their brightest in the winter months. Soft yellow dead nettle flowers appear in spring and are pleasant enough, but the dead spikes mar the beauty of the plant and are best cut off immediately the flowers are over.

By these standards *Lamium maculatum* is a reserved and modest plant but even so it quickly makes a wide mat of solid foliage which remains in good condition throughout the year. This plant sends out more restrained runners and is safe enough to use in the border. The sage green leaves have a median white stripe which makes a telling background for the magenta flowers. This species has a long flowering season and in mild winters will give a display of its hooded flowers. Bees seem to love it and visit the blooms time and time again. The profuse magenta flowers can be rather hard in some colour schemes, but for a softer effect the varieties *alba* and *roseum* can be used, the latter being a beautiful clear pink.

The only garden nettle which can be rather fussy and demanding is the beautiful golden form. This prefers a cool and moist site but when properly grown presents a pool of pure gold splashed with the usual white stripes. *Lamium orvala* is an imposing plant for a nettle; with erect stems topped by fine wine-coloured flowers, it is one of the clump-forming species that does not spread.

Primrose Family

One of the nicer aspects of growing the smaller kinds of primrose is that they are so good for planting in odd corners where few other colourful plants would survive. Grown informally between larger plants or crammed into crevices at the edge of a path they will thrive and make thick clumps studded with rich colour.

Regimented rows in full sun is the worst possible way of growing any primrose and they will never give as full a colour value as when grown in half shade. The magenta commoner Wanda can be an absolute treasure when used informally, poking out beneath a hedge or at the foot of a shady wall.

There is a great diversity of leaf colour and texture in the primulas between species like *P. sieboldii* with soft green, deeply crinkled leaves, Garryarde Guinevere whose leaves are deepest bronze and the neat rosettes of *P. marginata*. Most of the small species are easy to grow although there are a few exceptions, including the doubles which require more skill and constant division. A moist rich soil that is inclined to be heavy should ensure success with these.

The primrose family is an immense one; and while most of the larger Asian species are specialist plants and demand water in the garden, it is possible to build up a large collection of the smaller kinds under ordinary garden conditions

The centuries old hose-in-hose and Jack-in-the-green types are still available and worth a place in any collection. Of the old double primroses the easiest to grow are the white and the mauve and the two named varieties, Marie Crousse and Tyrian Purple. All are charming and showy spring flowers but without some attention even the so-called easy ones are apt to dwindle over the years until they are finally lost.

Spring

The early flowering *juliae* group has small round leaves and short stemmed single flowers that stand barely 2in above the ground. These will give a colourful display and are well suited for growing between more substantial evergreen border plants which will also give them some protection from the sun.

Birds will sometimes attack the flowers pulling the petals to pieces in an apparently senseless manner. The attraction is however the nectar at the base of the flower tubes and while black thread or some of the modern bird deterrents are partially effective they are usually so unsightly as to destroy the beauty of the plants.

Wood Lilies

Considering the beauty and comparative ease of culture of the wood lilies, it is surprising how rarely they are seen outside botanic gardens where usually a few of the thirty odd species are grown. Indeed only a few varieties are available to the gardener; but if one has *Trillium grandiflorum* (the Wake Robin) or one of its forms suffused with pink it is doubtful if either of these could be bettered as a woodland plant. Originating in the woods of north and eastern America they demand similar situations in the garden, and if woodland cannot be provided a moist shrubbery with plenty of peat and leaf mould should make a good home for them. Provided the soil conditions are satisfactory, it is possible to grow them in an open border; but the soil must be continuously moist, for a hot dry position will mean almost certain failure. Shady slopes at the base of rockeries also make good sites and provide an ideal show place for the beautiful three-petalled blooms which give the plant the name of Trinity Flower.

A less conspicuous trillium is one sometimes known as the Toad Lily, *T. sessile*. This has maroon flowers but its marbled grey leaves makes it a foliage plant of considerable attraction.

The dwarf of the family is *T. nivale* but it is very rare in cultivation. Not more than 6in high with white flowers, it makes a first-class rockery plant and is the one variety that will stand a dry soil and can be planted in a more elevated position.

Arisaemas

For similar situations, and those with a taste for the curious, the rarely seen arisaemas, those strange and handsome plants, are reasonably easy to grow. The most commonly known is probably Jack-in-the-Pulpit, *A. triphyllum*; although of bizarre appearance it is a very good plant. Given a moist woodland soil it will do well in most gardens, growing to about a foot high. This variety from north eastern America has a striking flower consisting of a spathe, pale green outside and marked with purple-brown lines inside. This spathe contains a brown spotted spadix which if one is lucky will sometimes produce scarlet berries in the autumn. Long stalked leaves which are divided into three segments flank the flower and remain in beauty for the rest of the summer. The leaves are so fine and unusual that it would be worth growing for these alone.

A fine hardy variety which can be seen in shady corners in the rock garden at Kew is *A. candidissimum*. This has larger tri-foliate leaves and a tubular white spathe tinted with pink and white lines. These are most effective seen against the large light green leaves.

The hardy varieties have a good range of colour and many of the combinations are as unusual as the flower shape. *A. japonicum* sports a green and white striped spathe. A rare but obtainable plant is *A. sikokiana* from Japan. This has purple and green bands with a strong purple line outside. The green and purple flecked centre holds a white spadix with a crimson stem. In spite of its rarity this is reputedly an easily grown plant with flowers that last for a long time. Another rarity is *A. wallichianum* from Kashmir. This has quite spectacular colouring of light and dark green on a ribbed spathe. The contrasting purple centre is chequered and veined with pale green and has a protruding dark spadix.

A charming dwarf suitable for a cool pocket in a rock garden, *A. ringens*, increases slowly over the years and makes a pleasing group.

Most of the arisaemas do not start into growth until quite late in the spring, usually not until May; but their divided leaves and fascinating flowers come at a time when plants of quiet interest are welcome among the brighter colours of early summer.

3

Summer

The changing shape, outline and colour accent of a well planted garden is one of the sustaining delights of the growing season. Plants come and go in their season of bloom with remarkable rapidity and the problem of keeping borders well furnished with flowers is one that needs careful planning to avoid mid-season gaps.

Those that give a blaze of colour in early summer and then leave an awkward space for the remainder of the season are only too familiar and are seldom dealt with as effectively as they might be. Usually the offending plants are the popular favourites that most gardeners would not be without, oriental poppies, lupins and delphiniums, all plants that take up a fair amount of space. So many of these early plants die badly and the obvious way of dealing with unsightly gaps is to mask the spent plant with another which does not make too much growth until the early summer.

Plants with wide branching heads such as gypsophila, phlox,

potentillas and some of the asters will soon screen the offending space and give a further pool of colour later in the season. The phloxes in particular are splendid mid-season standbys with a wide range of colour to suit any planting. As fill-in plants almost any position will suit them but they are one of the first plants to show signs of drought and must have adequate and constant moisture at the roots.

Other indispensable early summer plants like the peonies with their short season of bloom have decorative leaves that improve as the season progresses and can, if carefully planted, act as a foil to the bright colours of adjacent plants.

The practice of growing one of the more restrained clematis into a spent shrub or rose to extend the season of interest and colour is gaining favour. There is no reason why this innovation should not be applied to peonies. With the help of a few unobtrusive pea sticks to give height, the strong leaves of the larger peonies could make a wonderful background for any of the viticella clematis such as Huldine, Lady Betty Balfour or Ville de Lyon.

Clematis do not necessarily need to be grown vertically. Where wide gaps have to be covered they can be allowed to sprawl at ground level or mounded over chicken wire to give shape to the border. This is a good way of adding colour to the winter flowering heathers which can be a trifle dull in the summer months. Since heathers are normally planted in wide drifts the sprawling habit of the clematis lends itself admirably to this sort of gardening.

Honeysuckles, including the non-flowering golden reticulated form, can be used as an instant gap filler. Trained up a pole in the normal way they can be let down to ground level at the appointed time. They are however best not intermingled with other plants as their substantial growth might exclude light and air from the host plant, besides which they cannot be dealt with so easily as clematis at the end of the season.

Summary

Shade

In summers when we have more than our normal ration of sun, any shady spots in the garden are more than welcome. A well grown specimen tree with spreading branches sited on a lawn to give shade for one's leisure hours is one of the delights of the summer garden. Specimen trees with an umbrella-like spread such as catalpas and sophoras look well on any lawn or terrace. There are several trees of this shape which will not grow too quickly and are ideal for the small garden.

Running water is one of the coolest sounds and a delight in a garden where banks can be planted with lush moisture-loving plants. Few of us have this ideal condition, but a pond of still water reflecting the green of overhanging trees or a cloud across a blue sky will do much to strike a cool note. Most foliage plants which thrive at the waterside will enjoy shade and with their associations of moist and leafy soils they have a cool, fresh appearance.

Hostas, ferns and lilies love these conditions and will rarely burn in dappled sunlight. The large leaves of *Hosta glauca* are particularly cool, as are the spikes of mauve bells which are held above the platforms of leaves. Grown in shade, all hostas have fresh foliage although they reputedly do not flower as well there as in the sunshine. The variegated forms are also good in shade since the yellow markings remain in beauty for a longer period.

Lilies grown in full sun are a sorry sight compared with those grown in woodland conditions. Most varieties should be grown with their roots in the shade, but the whole plant prefers dappled sunshine. Even in a relatively open site much can be done by careful planting of a ground cover of cool green.

There is nothing worse than the sight of parched, cracked earth between plants. Groups of plants should be encouraged to overlap. As well as forming a sea of contrasting foliage, this ground cover will prevent the sun from drying out the ground beneath the plants and so conserve moisture. There are many plants with cool blue or glaucous foliage that revel in a hot dry soil. Some sedums and aceanas and most pinks are useful for breaking up areas of warm greens while the artemisias which also like sun and poor soil carry out the same role.

One of the loveliest of all foliage effects is that of *Rosa rubrifolia* with its glaucous and plum-coloured leaves and stems. This rose has small, attractive single flowers and handsome mahogany-coloured hips. The foliage is outstanding and makes an intriguing pool of soft colour which changes with the light. It is at its best in half light when it takes on amethyst tints.

Paved gardens can become hot if facing south or west but even the smallest space can be arranged with a ceiling of leaves. Some of the outdoor vines are ideal for this purpose and fruit well, as does Pinot Meunier whose jade green leaves are dusted with white.

The young leaves of this vine are edged with pink and are decorative in the growing season. The purple-leaved vine, *Vitis vinifera purpurea,* is also good particularly if grown with the golden-leaved hop, a fast growing climber which until recently, has been difficult to obtain.

Height

In the general froth and sea of summer flowers, a few carefully placed upright plants of striking proportions or architectural form are invaluable in giving accent and purpose to the design of a garden. Even in a well planned border furnished with the choicest foliage plants the outline will tend to be too soft without strong verticals to act as focusing points. A border planted with low subjects at the front and evenly banked with progressively taller things towards the back is usually unexciting to the eye but can be much more interesting if carefully broken up in bays and clumps.

Some of the medium sized fastigiate shrubs, particularly evergreens, will do this job permanently but where colour of a particular shape or texture is needed to compliment adjacent plantings plants with a rapid annual growth can be used. Dramatic effects can be arranged at the appropriate times with the simplest and easiest of plants. Groups of swiftly growing foxgloves are good in almost any setting and can be followed by even taller hollyhocks to carry on the theme of height through the season. Foxgloves are extraordinarily good in almost any setting, giving a long season of colour from their sturdy even spikes.

Having grown the double hollyhocks in a fairly wet year and been presented with the continually distressing sight of soggy, rotting and browning blooms, most gardeners sensibly revert to cultivating the less troublesome single varieties which are in any case far more beautiful with their silkier petals set off by a contrasting eye. Their one drawback as in all hollyhocks is the unsightly rust disease which seems to be more prevalent in country districts and once established is difficult to eradicate. Fungicides give some measure of control if applied frequently but are rarely completely effective.

Rivalling the hollyhocks in height the verbascums, with white woolly foliage and stems, are some of the most ornamental plants in the summer garden and will thrive in any well drained soil. These are mostly biennial and the most imposing of these is *V. bombyciferum,* sometimes listed as *V. broussa.* It has 8ft spikes of grey felted stems and leaves. The whole plant, leaves, stems and buds is densely clothed with silver hairs, the stems being studded with clear lemon flowers at the height of the season. This plant has the engaging habit of producing a few self-sown seedlings each year and like foxgloves will continue to appear in new places in subsequent years.

Most gardeners would not be without a good clump of delphiniums and for tall spires of blue there is nothing to match them. It is however a most uncommon sight to see these grown to perfection. There are so many hazards that even the most watchful gardeners are often defeated. Slugs like nothing better than the soft young shoots as they appear above the ground early in the year and from then on it is a constant battle against wind, rain and over-boisterous pets. In giving them enough support, staking has to be carried out with such severity that the whole beauty of the plant is lost and even then such measures are not always foolproof.

The taller kniphofias of late summer show no such failing and rarely need any form of support. There are now many superior medium sized cultivars obtainable which are useful for front and mid-border work but the older taller forms like *K. uvaria* still have a place where height is needed.

Another back-of-the-border plant which is too rarely seen is the khaki-coloured Plume Poppy, *Macleaya macrocarpa*. Together with its cultivar Coral Plume, it is a splendid plant for a neutral background effect and though the starry flowers are small the general effect of 6ft stems clothed with large lobed leaves of delicate colour is good. Running roots are the only drawback, but their progress is not rapid and so it is much less troublesome than acanthus, another plant that will raise itself above its neighbours with spikes of pink and purple flowers in grey bracts.

Angelica is a tall herb of great architectural value. This accommodating plant has stout stems clothed with handsome compound leaves and will reach a height of 5ft. The many umbels of white flowers are well shaped and the whole plant like many of the tall subjects has a fine outline which justifies a good position and background.

63

Peonies

As spring merges into summer the peonies, which for many people are the highlight of the garden are at their best. In spite of their comparatively short season of bloom the peony remains one of our favourite flowers although by planting various species and hybrids the season can be extended well into summer.

In May and early June when gardens have begun to overflow with thundery lilacs and dazzling viburnums the early flowering peonies hold the scene by sheer brilliance of colour. For outright show and excellence of foliage both the herbaceous and shrubby kinds have a place in most gardens and with the number of varieties available today the choice is wide.

Were its blooms not so fleeting it would surely vie with the rose in popularity, for its brilliance of colour and sumptuousness of form is rivalled by few other flowers. The robust old cottage varieties always look good, seemingly bursting with health, but some of the less common and more fragile species are occasionally subject to wilt and blind buds when whole stems will shrivel and die.

If planted with care in well prepared soil and not disturbed the life of the peony will most likely outlast that of the planter. They associate well with most other plants and are not fussy about soil or situation though many gardeners prefer to grow them in semi-shade. Indeed the tree peonies look well at the edge of a shrubbery and benefit by the protection of the surroundings from damaging winds.

The growth of most kinds starts very early and unless some form of protection is given, damage to shoots by frost and cold winds is inevitable. Young shoots of the tree peonies in particular are rather brittle and coming at a time of the year when we can expect strong winds, they deserve every protection.

Probably one of the most beautiful, is *P. suffruticosa,* the tree peony from China. The huge white single flowers have a central zone of maroon from which springs a boss of golden stamens and the deeply divided leaves are as handsome as any. This plant will stand some lime and can be grown in a large pot where it will thrive if well fed.

The shrubby peonies have a reputation for rather slow growth but with a rich diet and an occasional mulch a satisfactory rate of growth can be expected.

Eventually they need a good deal of space when fully grown but even small specimens will flower well when settled down after planting. These deciduous shrubby plants are extremely hardy and will build up over the years into plants 5ft high and wide, covered with satiny blooms the size of saucers.

Of the two other shrubby species, *P. lutea ludlowii* has light green leaves and clusters of golden cup-like flowers and is the fastest grower of all. The foliage of the delavayi hybrids has a metallic leaden quality of its own and contrasts well with other shrubs. Their flowers range from maroon to red and appear as the leaves are unfolding.

Hybrid tree peonies sometimes listed as Chinese or French varieties are magnificent creations with a wide range of colour and shape and are an ideal setting for other smaller foliage plants. The doubles are full blown and in shape rival the best of the old roses.

Some gardeners will prefer to grow some of the early flowering herbaceous species and this group are invaluable for the small border.

P. officinalis and its varieties is still one of the favourites and this old cottage-garden plant remains in leafy beauty throughout the summer. A very early flowering form, *P. tenuifolia* has foliage that is so finely cut that it might be that of fennel. The large deep crimson flowers with yellow stamens show up well against the light green leaves.

Flowering a little later *P. mlokosewitschii,* more easily remembered as Molly the Witch, is a first-class garden plant. The yellow blooms may be rather fleeting but they are numerous and the linings of the seed pods which follow are magenta and open up to display rows of black seeds. In autumn the leaves colour well making it a valuable plant throughout the growing season.

P. cambessedesii is rather tender but it is worth growing against a warm wall for its metallic blue foliage and rose pink flowers. This is another type that has brilliant seed pods to add colour to the summer garden.

All peonies like to feed well and will repay with masses of flowers if given a handful of bonemeal and a mulch of compost when the dead leaves are tidied up in the autumn. Herbaceous species and hybrids can give magnificent shows of bloom when grown with care, although the weight of the flower heads makes it advisable to twig with pea sticks early in the season. With many plants double forms are often regarded as inferior to the type but with double peonies the large blooms loosely filled with soft petals have an attraction of their own.

Those cultivars like Bowl of Beauty or Gleam of Light whose cups are filled with huge bosses of golden stamens add another facet to the peonies' many forms.

Most garden literature on the peony emphasises its longevity, ease of culture and trouble-free qualities, but like most plants they do appreciate clean conditions and a good diet. The trouble-free aspect should not deteriorate into neglect.

Irises

The month of May presents the gardener with some of the most colourful and flamboyant flowers of the year; and, like the peony, the iris in its various forms has several good early summer flowering species to offer. Rarely do they fail to provide a magnificent if rather fleeting display of brilliant silky blooms.

There are few gardens without one form or another of the bearded iris, usually the common *I. germanica,* which now offers a wide range of colour in the standards and falls. The faultless form and superb colouring of these flags are extremely tempting but in the average size garden there will not be space for more than a few cultivars since they have little to offer after flowering. The leaves which are superb at the height of the season slowly deteriorate and become rather unsightly by the end of the summer. Like most irises these revel in full sun and are never better than when planted among brick or stone where their rhizomes can get the full benefit of the reflected sun.

The foliage of that other tall iris, *I. pallida dalmatica,* retains its leaves in beauty throughout the summer. These are a clean and attractive glaucous green, a magnificent base for the fragrant lavender blue and golden flowers. The variegated form has some of the most striking leaves of all, broadly edged with creamy-white against the typical grey-green.

Iris pseudacorous also has a spectacular variegated form with huge 3ft leaves that are at their best when planted at the waterside. As the season progresses the variegation diminishes; but as an early summer subject where broad sword shaped leaves are required, this plant is unrivalled.

For weed proof ground cover at the waterside, *I. sibirica* builds up over the years into solid clumps with thickly matted roots that deter all but the most pernicious weeds. In spite of its tough and robust character this is an elegant plant with tall slender stems giving a succession of showy flowers of which there are white, blue and purple forms.

Another iris that demands moist soil or shallow water for a home is *I. laevigata,* a medium size plant that has various coloured forms. The pristine alba or the one with deep blue petals with a white streak are delightful plants giving a remarkable clean effect.

Few catalogues list the showy Japanese *I. kaempferi*. This is one of the few irises that demand an acid soil and ample moisture. If one can provide the right situation it is one of the most sumptuous of all, with large self-coloured or netted blooms of superb velvety texture.

The hybrid Monspur is an even taller plant of stately proportions and large enough to hold its own in the mixed border among shrubs and roses. The mauve standard and yellow falls are intricately veined and for the best results this is a plant worth good soil and a place in full sun.

If only it were possible to protect the leaves of *I. japonica* efficiently from the depredations of slugs and snails they would provide some of the finest evergreen foliage in the border. Formed in broad fans of shining green the leaves arch gracefully from the central rootstock and in early May send up thin wands punctuated with small orchid-like flowers. Ledger's variety is the best form of this particular iris with white fringed flowers delicately marked with blue and yellow. Planting instructions are somewhat confused, some catalogues advocating shade and others sun but from experience in trying both sites, established clumps under a south or west wall will usually send up a dozen or so flower spikes. In this position there is also considerably less damage from snails.

It would be interesting to see the Japanese roof iris *I. tectorum* grown in thatch but at ground level it is undoubtedly easier to appreciate the detail and outline of its beautiful flowers. In Japan this early summer bloomer seeds itself in the thatch of country houses. The type has lilac flowers with crests marked with white standing well above light green leaves. A pure white form alba, is also obtainable and is exceptionally good, doing best in a hot sunny position; ample moisture is needed in the growing season.

Page 69   9 *For bold foliage effects there are no better plants than the* hostas. H. albo picta *has yellow and green variegations which fade to green in late summer*
10 *Pulmonarias have handsome spotted leaves. In this form the silver spots are so dense that they merge together*

Page 70 11 *A spectacular blue grass,* Helictotrichon sempervirens, *makes a compact clump with arching 4ft flower stems*

12 *The yellow stripes and purple flowers of* Molina caerulea variegata *make this one of the most charming and colourful grasses*

During the early summer the beautiful but modest yellow and purple flowers of the Gladwin Iris, *I. foetidissima,* often go unnoticed among the more colourful plants. A more startling show is given for many weeks in the autumn when the huge seed pods split to show rows of scarlet seeds. These do not fall from the pod immediately and a splendid display can be had well into the winter. As cutting material for the house in winter they are superb especially if given a light coating of gum to keep the seeds in place. This is one of the easiest plants to grow, thriving in any soil with shining evergreen leaves that always look good. A Chinese form of this species that is obtainable from some nurseries is larger and superior in all its parts. The variegated form does not flower so freely but has such good leaves at all times of the year that it is one of the best foliage plants for any situation.

Crown Imperial

One of the oldest plants, and also as its name implies one of the most stately, is the Crown Imperial. This large fritillary is a native of Persia and the Himalayas and was a favourite cultivated plant in Turkish gardens. It reached England by the late sixteenth century and since then has been a great favourite and once settled happily in a garden should stay there for many years.

For some gardeners with sensitive noses this plant has a drawback, it has a decidedly foxy smell and is not suitable as a cut plant for the house. Others complain that they are difficult to grow; but the secret of success is in the planting. A rich deep loam seems preferable with some coarse sand for sharp drainage and the initial planting should be made in very early spring. If planted in the autumn before a wet winter, the bulb may well rot. Some nurserymen advise planting the bulbs on the side so that water will not lie in the hollow at the top. Groups of three or five are worth an important place in the border when little else has grown to such bold proportions. The stout 3ft stems are surmounted by a circular cluster of drooping bells surmounted by a crown of leaves. The two better known forms are the red and the yellow, but bronze and orange flowered forms can be obtained.

Such was the fascination of these plants that a dozen or more varieties were in cultivation towards the end of the eighteenth century, some with double flowers and others with gold or silver variegation to the leaves. Another is said to have had a supplementary whorl of flowers; but like many of the old and treasured plants few survive today, probably because they did not possess the excellent constitution of their commoner relatives.

As a flower of legend, the early gardening writers rarely failed to emphasise the interpretations which might be placed on the pearl-like drops of water at the base of each bell. Although the flowers are pendant and droop at an acute angle this nectar will not fall out even if the plants are sharply shaken but if removed artificially will quickly re-form in order to nourish the seedhead. The seedheads which are large and as striking as the flowers in architectural beauty will dry well for indoor decoration.

Pinks

There can be few gardens which do not have favourite clumps of pinks that have originated as pipings gratefully received from generous gardeners. The old pinks certainly come into this category, those known as Painted Ladies or the laced pinks are much sought after and too seldom found in nursery catalogues. The patternings, fringings and edgings of these easy-going cottage garden plants rarely fail to excite admiration; although the exquisite fragrance of these plants has always been regarded as of prime importance. That magnificent if somewhat untidy nineteenth-century pink, Mrs Sinkins, which frequently bursts its calyx, has an overpowering and cloying perfume that is not found in blooms of more perfect form.

Scanning lists of pinks that have been fashionable through the centuries from the Sops-in-Wine in Chaucer's day, to Nonsuch and Painted Lady of Tudor times through to the still popular Sam Barlow and Emile Pare of the nineteenth century one realises how few of these have survived and are readily available to the gardener. The oldest, Sops-in-Wine, is said to still survive in a few Berkshire cottage gardens, as does Fenbow, the Nutmeg Clove of approximately the same date.

The clove-scented Bat's Double Red raised in London in the seventeenth century is still listed in at least one catalogue. This richly coloured pink bears flowers on 12in stems over a long period. Another old plant still listed is the silvery pink Inchmery with double blooms on 9in stems, a useful height for picking and unlikely to suffer too badly in rough weather.

Fringed pinks also have great charm and assort well in mixed plantings. Some named varieties are still available. Bridal Veil and Fimbriata, two of the old ones are still sold, both are good whites, the former having a crimson blotch at the base of each petal. That outstanding pink raised in Orleans, Emile Pare, which shows evidence of the sweet william in its ancestry, will usually flower itself to death after a few years and is best perpetuated by propagating a few cuttings each year. Its clusters of double salmon pink flowers are held well above good foliage of the softest green.

Most of the modern hybrid pinks have all the charm of the older forms with the added advantage of a much longer flowering period. These extremely hardy pinks offer a wide range of colour and flower continuously through summer and autumn. With their short stems they need little attention and make splendid edgings in any border that gets its fair share of sun. These hybrids are capable of producing an enormous number of flowers throughout

73

the season, the variety Doris being outstanding for its long flowering period. Some authorities favour the practice of thinning out the flowering stems in spring to conserve the strength of the plant. All pinks root easily from cuttings or layers taken in June or early July. Once rooted they quickly make sturdy plants and stopping is essential in the early stages in order to produce well-shaped clumps. While pinks will certainly thrive in limey soils of poor texture they do need to be occasionally fed to support the huge flower crop. Coarse hoof and horn or bonemeal dressed on the soil will keep them in good condition for several years.

Lilies

With many perennials it is preferable to plant in the early spring when the worst of the winter weather is over and the roots are again becoming active. There are other plants that are practically indestructible and can be planted or divided in autumn, winter or spring, provided the ground is not frozen hard. One of these is the Hemerocallis or Day Lily, a plant that will begin flowering in June and continue for weeks on end. Some of its varieties have a delicious fragrance. In February their light green grassy leaves pierce the soil and by the time that the first spring flowers are in bloom, they will be solid enough to provide a pleasing background and good ground cover.

The flowering period of the various cultivars ranges from spring to late summer, the waxy blooms being produced on stout leafless stems that are very tough and need no staking. The individual lily-shaped flowers last for one day only giving rise to the name 'Day Lily' but the succession of flowers goes on for a long time and by growing a few carefully chosen varieties the season can be prolonged by several weeks.

The traditional colours of the Day Lily have until recent

years been rather restricted, ranging from buff, yellow through orange and copper to deep mahogany red. Lately, particularly in America, great improvements have been made by the hybridists and various shades of pink are now added to the list. The variety Pink Damask is probably the best of these generally available.

These long lived plants are useful in any border or awkward corner and will succeed in sun or shade providing the ground remains reasonably moist. Some authorities advise leaving clumps undisturbed and applying an annual top dressing of fertiliser or compost but for really free-flowering specimens it is probably best to divide the clumps occasionally. This is an almost infallible remedy when blooms become sparse although it usually takes a year for the plant to recover. This plant is virtually disease free.

The eremurus is an aristocrat of the summer border and known as the foxtail lily but is quite unlike any other of that clan. It is an uncommon plant and rarely fails to cause comment when seen towering above its neighbours. This is a plant that should be installed in the autumn but rather more care is needed in the actual planting operation for its thick roots which radiate rather like the rays of a starfish are extremely brittle and very easily damaged. It is also advisable to give it a position with some shelter from the wind to protect the flowering spires from summer gales. The background of a dark hedge or wall will help to accentuate their subtle colours of pale pink, yellow, fawn and white all of which are suffused with green. These curious colours are most attractive, especially when seen as an 8ft spike of flower which is the size one can expect from the larger varieties such as *E. robustus* or *E. elwesii*. For smaller settings it is possible to get less exuberant varieties, *E. Bungei* and *E. olgae,* growing to 2ft and 4ft respectively.

Geraniums

There are too few good garden plants which can be truthfully recommended as trouble free, virtually disease resistant and with an aptitude to grow well in most situations. The family of hardy herbaceous geraniums is a large one that fulfils all these conditions with over a score of good garden varieties suitable for most positions. When planting out all these geraniums can be considered in two categories, those that are restrained enough to be allowed into the more formal parts of the garden and those that reproduce too generously and are best confined to the wilder parts.

In the former category the largest and grandest is *G. armenum,* a 3ft plant with shiny magenta flowers and a startling black eye. These are set above a clump of deeply cut leaves and the plant is worth a good place in any border, preferably in full sun.

The one that is always in flower and a firm favourite is *G. endressii.* This is the most adaptable of all geraniums and is not particular about soil or situations. The silvery pink flowers and fresh green leaves have a remarkably clean appearance and is a good weed suppressor when massed. The only attention that geraniums require during the growing season is dead heading. This is important and in many cases will encourage the plant to give a finer second crop of flowers. All geraniums have good leaf shapes and if kept tidy will make decorative hummocks of green in their own right.

The two varieties *G. macrorrhizum* and *G. renardii* have some of the finest leaves of all. The rounded foliage of the former is a good crisp green that takes on intense shades in late summer culminating in bright autumn tints. Although its flowering season is limited, the blooms are quite unlike those of any other geranium and are held well above the platform of leaves on strong crimson stalks. There are several colour variants, deep rose, pink and white. The latter is a most pleasing form with its white petals clasped by red calyces. In favoured localities or warm corners the leaves are almost evergreen and as fragrant as any herb. Once established it is completely weed proof and fits in happily with any planting scheme.

The clump forming *G. renardii* spreads much more slowly and is best planted in full sun. Deep veins crimp the rounded sage green leaves which make a perfect background for the display of white flowers which are splashed and veined with purple.

The smallest geranium commonly seen is the cerise *G. sanguineum*. This is good for the front of the border since it is rarely out of flower, but its less vigorous form *G. s. lancastriense* is a wiser choice for the rock garden. Its pale pink flowers and neat habit assort well with choicer subjects and will not overrun them. Ballerina is another refined form with more colourful flowers.

Most forms of *G. pratense* and *G. nodosum* are inveterate seeders and are best left to the wilder parts of the garden where they can colonise at will. The double forms of *G. pratense* do not have this distressing habit but the single blooms are almost luminous blue and seen at their best in the dappled light of thin woodland.

Once *G. nodosum* begins to flower the succession of lilac pink blooms is endless. It has, however, atrocious seeding habits, the seedlings having long wiry roots that can be difficult to remove. These seem to delight in germinating in the centre of a clump of some favourite flower. Worse still, they will try to find protection at the base of the most spiny roses and defy all attempts at complete removal. There is no mistaking the leaves of this species, even in the seedlings, for they are as attractive as they are tenacious. Shiny and lobed with a newly varnished appearance they should be eliminated from the more formal parts of the garden as soon as they are detected.

Summer

Poppies

One of the most sumptuous effects possible in the summer garden is that of a sturdy clump of well-grown oriental poppies. *Papaver orientale* has a comparatively short flowering season; its untidy habit when dying down makes it essential to replant the area or disguise the effect quickly. With established clumps the foliage can be cut right down to the ground, the soil lightly forked over and replanted with quick growing late summer plants like dahlias.

In the smaller garden they are best planted as a generous clump in a mid-border position where the business of covering-up is made easier. Being soundly perennial it is possible to cover their crowns with some wide-spreading or roving plants such as *Clematis integrifolia, Tropaeolum speciosum* or the grey leaved shrubby *Artemesia absinthum.* At the height of its season the foliage plays no mean part in the general decorative effectiveness of the plant. The divided leaves clothed with minute hairs give a feathery effect and their deep green colour is an ideal background to the glowing red petals.

In a deep well-drained soil the oriental poppies will last for many years. To retain the vigour of the plant their healthy appetite demands a generous mulch of compost round the crowns in early spring. When growth begins it is fairly rapid and the plants should be discreetly twigged. Some varieties tend to sprawl and heavy rain plays havoc with the sturdiest plants when heavy with bud and flower.

The single blood-red flowers of the type stained with a black blotch at the base of each petal is by far the best and seemingly favourite form but colour breaks in other shades and double forms are available. For those who find the red form too strong, the cultivar Perry's White is an alternative worth considering. The huge white petals are decorated by a deep maroon blotch at the base and this is a much more refined and useful form for cool plantings. This is an easy plant to propagate by root cuttings. These are so easy that when plants are lifted and the fleshy roots broken the pieces left in the ground will usually develop into individual plants and will take some time to eradicate. Varieties of a similar plant, *Papaver bracteatum*, have the same showy qualities but have leafy stems as opposed to bare hairy stems of *P. orientale*.

Clematis

Herbaceous varieties of clematis are less frequently seen than the climbing types but they are good border plants, and ideal for filling in gaps left by earlier flowering things like the poppies. There are several forms of *C. heracleifolia* all with fragrant hyacinth-like flowers. The variety *C. Davidiana* is truly herbaceous and its 2ft or so of growth requires no staking. For much of their length the strong leafy stems bear clusters of light blue flowers from July to September. This plant is not at all particular about soil, but should be given a sunny situation in the middle of the border.

In the mixed border it is one of the most suitable plants for associating with roses, especially pinks or whites such as Louise Odier or Iceberg. By late summer the leaves of this variety turn an attractive yellow before the plant is cut back by the first frosts.

For an earlier display in June and July, *C. recta* will make an upright bushy plant with inch wide white flowers in branching sprays. This form can make a large bushy plant and like many of the climbing members of this family, will do well in chalk soils. While it has a fairly erect habit, it is advisable to insert a few strong twiggy sticks round the plant for support so that it will not collapse under the weight of the rain-sodden blooms. A double form of this plant is listed but rarely seen.

The most delicate in appearance of these herbaceous forms is *C. integrifolia* with deep blue flowers, bearing reflexed petals like Turks Cap lilies. These pendulous blooms are almost indigo in colour having purple sheen in some lights. This plant will grow flat along the ground, but for space saving in the small garden, it can be persuaded to grow up sticks or be given a living support and allowed to climb up through a small shrub. This is by far the most natural way to treat this plant since its stems are brittle and must be allowed to grow in their own way. Any attempts to train by hand or tie back individual stems usually results in an unnatural mass punctuated by broken stems.

Onions

There is no doubt that if handled excessively some of the decorative onions can so impregnate the hands with their garlic smell that it takes days to disappear. For this reason alone many gardeners despise and neglect these fine and easy plants. Even that great gardener William Robinson had little good to say of them in his book *The English Flower Garden*, grudgingly mentioning only a few of 'possible garden value'. The garlic smell is in fact only evident when the stems or bulbs are crushed or broken and this should rarely happen if planted well away from paths.

In spite of this dislike by some gardeners, decorative onions have been grown in our gardens for many years surviving the changes of gardening fashion. In Elizabethan times they were known as Mollies, since the main variety then grown was *Allium moly*, the one with bright yellow flowers. This species can spread rapidly and is best for naturalising in the wild garden in sun or light shade. The only one that is so invasive as to become troublesome is *A. vineale,* the crow garlic but this is unlikely to be listed in any reputable catalogue. Other varieties to be found in nurserymen's lists range from the 6in rose coloured *A. ostrowskianum* for rockeries to the 5ft *A. giganteum.* Dry sandy soils are preferable for the best results according to most authorities. The only fault with the large varieties is that they do not need staking as the globular heads become heavy—particularly after rain.

An early flowering, low growing onion that catches every eye is *A. karataviense.* This has broad glaucous leaves and large spherical flower heads that lie on the ground in clusters and are a substantial addition to any spring planting. Some of the most spectacular heads are like bursting rockets and after the flowering period are no less impressive in seed. A striking one in this group is *A. albo pilosum* growing to 2ft and having individual star-shaped lilac pink flowers in June.

One of the most sought after forms, *A. siculum,* has a distinctly different habit and is hung with ivory bells stained with green and maroon markings. The flowering cycle is one of the most interesting of all plants. Beginning with a cluster of upright buds encased in a transparent membrane, the flowers develop into an arrangement of pendant bells. After fertilisation the seedheads stiffen up and remain for many weeks like a cluster of upright rockets. This onion will occasionally rest after flowering and not bloom again until the second year, but seedlings frequently germinate and establish to build up a succession of flowering bulbs.

The common chives of the kitchen garden, *A. schoenoprasum,* make a good edging plant especially if the giant variety can be obtained. This plant grows in tufts rather like spring onions, as does Chinese chives, *A. tuberosum,* another good edging plant with white blooms. As can be seen the decorative onions are a versatile lot, and include, for collectors of the curious, that amusing plant *A. bulbiferum* which produces its young in the form of bulbs at the top of the flowering stem.

Herbs

There is for many gardeners a fascination about growing herbs and constructing herb gardens as a decorative element. Even when comparatively few herbs are used in the kitchen the desire to cultivate some of the less common kinds is spurred on by their decorative and aromatic qualities and by their usefulness as border plants. Most have foliage as pleasing as any herbaceous plant and are not particular as to soil and situation as long as it is fairly sunny and does not dry out too quickly. The low creeping thyme and marjoram are excellent for growing at the edge of stone paths or steps where one can get the full benefit of the aromatic foliage and the leaves will soften the edges of the hardest stone.

Rampant spreaders like mint need to be contained if the herb garden is to remain neat but this can be achieved without too much difficulty, by sinking a bottomless bucket or container flush with the level of the soil to restrict the roots.

Today there are a number of decorative culinary mints available and one of the very best for a patch of light colour is a planting of the variegated mint, *Mentha rotundifolia variegata*. The foliage colours are an exquisite apple green offset by splashes of white and cream. Its vigour equals that of any of the mint family and its delicious fragrance surpasses any other herb. This is a plant to be grown at the edge of a path, where it can be brushed against, causing its scent to rise in clouds and carry for yards. The flowers are of no great decorative value and are best pinched out to keep the plant as a compact hummock.

Another good family of plants to grow at the edge of a path

are the marjorams. It is more fashionable these days to grow the golden marjoram, *Origanum vulgare aureum,* a good plant requiring little care and rarely exceeding its allotted space. The new foliage which appears in early spring makes a mat of brilliant golden yellow and retains its colour until well into the summer. The common pot marjoram should not be despised as a decorative plant since its tiny blooms are pleasing in bud, flower and seed. These are borne on wiry stems a foot above a mat of dark green leaves. The whole plant is tough and wiry and will grow satisfactorily in the most unpromising places.

The ordinary green leaved balm is a pleasant enough plant if not very striking. Its variegated form however has leaves that never fail to catch the eye, the markings being gold against dark green. Although easy enough to grow, this is still rather a rare plant. Its leaves are at their best in early spring and early summer but at all times give off a strong lemon scent when bruised.

For height in the herb garden there is nothing to surpass the vaporous outline of fennel. The quality and texture of its leaves makes it rather difficult to place where it will show to best advantage. Both the green and bronze forms are very beautiful with finely cut foliage and umbels of yellow flowers. Fennel is a prolific seeder and the plant should be cut down before the seeds ripen. A good way of growing individual clumps is to cut the flowering stems out completely and rely on the foliage which gives a filmy smoky effect particularly beautiful after rain, when bejewelled by droplets.

Failure to remove the seedheads before they ripen inevitably results in a mass of seedlings which can be troublesome to eradicate once their long tap roots have gained a hold.

Myrrhis odorata, more commonly known as Sweet Cecily or the Sweet Fern as well as a host of other country names, is a graceful old cottage plant. Though seldom grown in the herb garden these days, it is still worth a place in a moist semi-shaded spot in the wild garden. The flowers and foliage are attractive to bees and it used to be the practice to rub the inside of the hive with the fragrant leaves to attract new swarms.

The umbels of white flowers rather like those of cow parsley are followed by large elongated black seeds which dry well and can be kept for winter decoration. They should, however, be removed from the plant before they fall, as its tendency to over-seed is its one disadvantage. The seedlings are quite distinctive and easily removed when young but rapidly develop long taproots. It is one of the easiest border plants to grow and the soft ferny leaves will appear above ground in early spring to give enjoyment for the whole season.

There is a surprising variety of leaf texture in the creeping forms of thyme from the dark green mats of *Serpyllum coccineum* to the woolly grey leaves of *T. s. lanuginosus* and the variegated and golden leaved cultivars. These are ideal for weaving between larger plants and are easily controlled by clipping and edging.

One of the strong points about growing herbs is their adapt-ability in fitting in with modern gardening trends. Most of them have distinctive and fragrant leaves and can be used as under-planting and companions to flowering shrubs and roses. The shrubby types of herbs are especially useful for this kind of situa-tion as they eventually become large enough to fend for themselves although their roots are shallow enough not to interfere with adjacent plantings. For shrub roses there can be no more trouble-free and weed-proof underplanting than the shrubby sages.

The English broad leaved form is effective enough but rarely flowers and should be substituted for the narrow leaved Spanish variety that carries masses of clear blue flowers which coincide with the midsummer roses. This one tends to become rather leggy towards the end of the season but responds well to severe pruning early in the year. The purple-leaved form which also flowers well is a magnificent foliage plant especially against roses with grey or light green leaves.

84

Filling a similar function the silver leaved cotton lavenders look good against the darker leaved roses. Unlike the old English lavender it is simple enough to prevent these from becoming leggy by cutting back to the previous year's growth in spring.

Purple and mauve flowering lavenders, are the very essence of high summer and delight in hot exposed positions. Again these look particularly well with roses and if some of the smaller and more compact varieties are planted they should need only a minimum of attention. This consists of the removal of the spent flowers and stalks after flowering and a light clipping in the spring. The cultivars Hidcote and Twickel Purple are both small shrubs with good form and extremely fragrant.

There are few small shrubs with good blue foliage and it is difficult to imagine anything surpassing the soft shades of Jackman's Blue Rue. While most herbs demand a sunny situation this amenable little shrub will put up with part shade. Grown well it will make a dense rounded bush of filigree foliage bearing curious small yellow flowers that are probably best cut off if one wants to retain an overall blue effect. A variegated rue, the best forms of which make a bold splash of cream, is becoming more easily available but it does not have the pleasing rounded form of the plain variety and unless carefully grown can be rather sparse.

The shrubby thymes add another welcome fragrance to the garden on a hot summer's day and the upright forms *T. citrio-dorus* and *T. nitidus* quickly make dense little bushes 10in or so high. Their minute leaves set on wiry stems are good the whole year through with several weeks of colour from the tiny lipped flowers. Hysopp too will add its pungent aroma to the garden but unfortunately tends to become lax and open in habit lacking the satisfactory density of the thyme.

The ease with which all these shrubby herbs strike from cuttings make them ideal plants for increasing and growing as low hedges for flower borders. Once rooted they make rapid growth and in a matter of months make sturdy plants ready for setting out.

With some, like the sages and lavenders, their one failing is that they grow rather too quickly and within two or three years take on a knarled and shapeless appearance. In certain positions in the garden this is acceptable but normally it is best to replace them with young plants when they have reached this stage.

No herb garden is complete without one rosemary shrub situated in the warmest possible spot. A south or west facing wall should ensure success and reliable spikes of mauve flowers in early spring. The ordinary rosemary can take up more than its fair share of space and for the small herb garden the form known as Miss Jessup's Upright is the one to choose. When growing well this makes a sturdy vertical shrub with a mass of deep mauve flowers.

Thistles

Of all the ornamental plants with thistle heads, the eryngiums are probably the most popular being mostly of manageable size and furnished with stout self-supporting stems. Their strong form and outlines are ideal for strengthening loose herbaceous plantings over a long period. Of the European species *E. gigan-teum* is the boldest of all. From a rosette of dark green basal leaves the branching stem rises to a height of 2ft and is set with stout thimble-like heads of steely blue flowers surrounded by pale spiny collars.

As the season progresses the whole plant fades to the colour of pale ivory and for this reason is sometimes known as Miss Will-mott's Ghost. This monocarpic plant will seed freely in most soils but since the seeds take eighteen months to germinate consecutive annual sowings should be made to begin with. Unwanted seedlings should be removed without delay, since once growing strongly, they quickly send down long taproots that are

Page 87 13 *The free*
flowering and fragrant
hybrid musk rose Felicia.
Shrub roses like this fit
naturally into mixed
plantings

14 *The shapely blooms of*
Mme Pierre Oger, a
Bourbon rose with perpetual
flowering habit and rich
fragrance

Page 88 15 *Of the herbaceous artemisias,* A. *Silver Queen is one of the best forms. Its weak stems require the support of adjacent plants*

16 *For a hot dry position* Stachys lanata *is a good low-growing grey plant. The variety Silver Carpet does not flower and makes labour saving ground cover*

difficult to remove without snapping off. This is one of the best thistles for winter decoration and will dry naturally *in situ*.

A similar sized plant, *E. alpinum,* is much more difficult to dry effectively, but the flowers have such attractively laced collars that one can hardly resist the temptation. For some reason this species is not so tenacious as the former and established clumps can disappear. Insufficient drainage might well be the reason for this since all eryngiums prefer an open or sandy soil.

Another good perennial eryngium is *E. bourgatii,* a plant with deeply cut basal foliage and blue-green flowers. The marbled evergreen rosettes of *E. variifolium* are handsome throughout the winter, and although the flowers are individually small their mass makes a satisfactory effect.

The larger evergreen South American species are not reliably hardy and resent the combination of moisture and frost so fiercely that they will rot away unless given liberal helpings of coarse sand beneath their leafy rosettes. When growing happily these are magnificent plants, forming wide mats of narrow spiny leaves from which rise branching stems 4ft or so in height set with the typical thimble-like flowers. Those of *E. bromeliifolium* are greenish white. The leaves of *E. pandanifolium* are the largest of all with jagged saw edges and the flowering stem can easily reach 10ft. For such a large plant the flowers are surprisingly small but have good form.

If a tall hardy spiky plant is needed there is nothing to surpass the Fullers Teasel, *Dipsacus fullonum.* This stately biennial is one of the easiest of all thistles to grow, its only fault being a tendency to overseed. The individual flower heads on branching stems are exceptionally strong and shapely in form, the individual mauve flowers first opening in a circle round the middle of the head. A metallic sheen covers the prickly stems which are extremely strong and completely self-supporting. This is another plant that dries well and a clump of these left standing can be a feature of the winter garden. The needle-sharp spines of the

F   89

cotton thistle, *Onopordon acanthium,* can be tolerated for the sake of the fine leaf shape and colour. Each year they offer a few self-sown seedlings, that can, if caught soon enough, be transplanted into their permanent position and grown on into towering giants of 6–8ft. This is another biennial plant that in the first year makes a handsome rosette of silver leaves and is decorative throughout the winter, looking good in all but the wettest weather.

In the early summer of its second year a magnificent fast growing flowering stem arises, branching as it grows. Both stems and branches are winged with sculptured flanges covered with fine silver down and edged with a sharp row of spines.

The typical thistle head flowers are a strong purplish blue and show well against the grey but should not be allowed to mature unless seed is required. Prompt dead heading will conserve the strength of the plant and its good looks should last well into the autumn.

Even where space is limited and only one plant can be grown at the back of the border, its height, colour and outline justify its inclusion. Grown in groups 2ft or so apart the lattice work of interlacing branches creates a silvery background to the rest of the border and provides mutual support for the group.

If one is not short of space in the border the cardoon, *Cynara cardunculus,* can make a magnificent spot plant. These have some of the most colourful thistle heads of all. They are a deep purple blue, encased in silvery scales held on branching 6ft stems. The large grey-green leaves are deeply cut and build up into a graceful mound. This is a strong and heavy plant and needs shelter from the wind and some staking.

On a smaller scale the annual *Cnicus diacantha* is worthy of cultivation in rough places if only for its geometrical rosettes of glossy leaves lined with silver markings and tipped with ivory spikes. More commonly known as the Blessed Thistle this plant will send up 2ft stems with clusters of yellow flowers.

The milk thistle, *Silybum marianum,* is another medium-sized plant with good variegated leaves but these are broad, deeply cut and undulating, armed with needle-like spines. The conspicuous white netting superimposed on glossy green makes this one of the most decorative plants of all when in its rosette stage. This thistle is easily raised from seed and will perpetuate itself in rough areas.

The rich green rosettes of the Himalayan thistle, *Morina longifolia*, are evergreen and good garden material at any time of the year but when the 3ft spikes of whorled flowers bloom in June and July it is transformed into the most elegant of garden plants. This is a choice plant and the pink and white flowers which are encased in sculptured bracts remain in beauty over a long period. As plants of elegant habit these benefit from being grown singly or in small groups. Only in this way can the full beauty and design of the plant be observed.

For the alpine garden, *Carlina acaulis*, is quite trustworthy and has the most fascinating and intricate flowers. Full sun and a fairly poor soil will suit this prostrate plant. In spite of its name the flowers of this plant are rarely stemless and are usually borne on stems 8 or 9in high. The central disc of the flower is pale ivory in colour, surrounded by long shapely bracts which last for many months.

Summer Bulbs

It is sad that so many of the summer flowering bulbs have failed to gain popularity. Winter and spring bulbs from the earliest snowdrops of January to the daffodils and tulips of April and May are planted unstintingly, but with the exception of the lilies too many of the others are neglected. Blooming in summer the smaller flowering kinds are not always successful when competing with bolder herbaceous plants, but most will find the conditions they prefer and add interest if planted between shrubs.

If the flowering period of the camassias occurred in a less leafy month they would be striking specimen plants and much sought after, but blooming as they do in June and early July bolder plants in the border tend to overshadow them. The camassia, or quamash, naturalises as easily as the daffodil and is best inter-planted in rough grass with other bulbs to extend the season of colour. The star-like flowers in various shades of blue and white are borne on 2ft spikes which rise way above the grassy leaves. If planted thickly enough the effect is good but it is probably better to concentrate on one colour for full impact.

A summer bulb that can hold its own in any border is *Galtonia candicans*, a tall and stately plant with pendulous white bells. The beauty of the individual flowers is enhanced by an edging of green, and a suffusion of the same colour at the base of each petal. The whole candelabra of flowers emits a subtle fragrance. Planted in sun against the grey foliage of artemisias or the blue leaves of rue or *Hosta glauca* this plant is at its best. After the flowers have faded, fine heads of angular seeds decorate the garden for many weeks.

Of the three really hardy species of Leucojum, *L. vernum* and *L. aestivum* flower from February to March and mid-April to May respectively, and *L. autumnale* which comes into bloom in September is an asset to any garden when given a warm position. It is rather more slender than the other snowflakes, and some would even call it spindly; but when happy with its position a few bulbs will spread over the years into a generous clump with pink tinted snowdrop-like flowers. Few of the summer flowering bluebells are good enough for garden work but one species, *Scilla peruviana*, makes up for the shortcomings of the rest of the family. The flowers are borne on stout stems in May and June and the whole plant is of a robust appearance capable of fending for itself in the border.

There are a number of other early summer flowering bluebells worthy of a place in the garden, including an uncommon variety

with the self-explanatory name of *S. autumnalis* which is supposed
to be a good seaside plant, with pinkish-lilac flowers that reach
their best in September.

The small crocus-like zephranthes from South Africa is also
worth trying; the hardiest species is *Zephranthes candida* with
cream flowers and orange stamens. It will usually survive the
winter if planted in a narrow strip under a south-facing wall.

For those who have a narrow border to fill under a south or
west wall and would like something exotic, the Mexican Tiger
Flower might well be tried. April is the month to plant the corms
of the *tigridia* as it is called botanically, and while the normal
practice is to lift these in the autumn, it has been found that it is
possible to overwinter them in their flowering positions. A
surprising number will come through unscathed provided that
they are planted at least 4in deep where normal frosts will not
touch them. If lifted they should be stored like gladioli in sand
or peatmoss. In the growing season they like a rich diet and ample
moisture in order to produce the wonderful spotted three-
petalled flowers. Like the day lilies the individual blooms last
in perfection for one day only but each stem carries six or more
buds. These develop into flowers 4in across ranging in colour
through red, pink, yellow and white; although the white is not
as vigorous as the coloured varieties.

Another exotic to fill a similar position is the *crinodenna*, a
hybrid between *Crinum moorei* and *Amaryllis belladonna*. The
result is a plant with the persistant leaves of the crinum and the
large trumpet-shaped flowers of the amaryllis. Again in a sheltered position in favoured districts this plant will survive several
winters out of doors. The flowers which appear in autumn last
well and are magnificent pink funnels about 4in across; when a
number of these can be induced to open together, they can be
the highlight of the garden.

A plant allied to the amaryllis and liking similar conditions,
Nerine bowdenii, is the only really hardy member of the nerines.

The bulbs once planted should not be disturbed untill he groups have become too congested by which time there will be a noticeable decrease in the number of flowers. The umbels of flowers are produced on stout stems, flower before the leaves have developed and have a remarkable iridescent quality in the petals. They are excellent plants for cutting, being both showy and long lasting.

Of the modern *Crinums*, the variety *powellii* is probably the hardiest and most commonly seen. This is a very fine hybrid with 2–3ft stems and large lily shaped flowers varying in colour from a deep pink to pure white. The bulbs again increase quite freely but should only be divided when necessary and then in spring. Flowers are produced from July to September, a period when few other bulbous plants of this size are in flower and since its season of beauty is such a long one, it can make an important pool of colour in the border.

Although all these plants are reasonably hardy, it is probably wise to give them a covering of bracken or ash to provide extra protection during severe spells.

Shade Loving Plants

Shady borders or semi-woodland provide the conditions that so many of our finest garden plants prefer. Among these are many of the more interesting, mostly of quiet colour and good leaf form.

Unobtrusive plants of quiet habit relying on intricacy of form and delicacy of colour for sustaining effect are all too uncommon in the summer border although many of them are easy enough to grow and worthy of wider recognition and use. Others have been so neglected that they are now only obtainable as choice plants from one or two specialist nurserymen. Some which were once thought to be of doubtful hardiness have long since proved themselves adaptable to varying climates, but are still regarded with suspicion by the unadventurous.

Probably the easiest and most prolific plants for quiet colour are the astrantias that will thrive in any soil and situation except a hot dry one. The symetrically intricate flowers of all the forms are borne in branching heads, each flower being composed of a dome of minute florets surrounded by a disc of showy bracts.

Astrantia major has a long flowering season. The first pearl-grey flowers appear in early summer and, providing the spent stems are removed, flowering will continue until autumn. Seen at its best in the garden against a dark background, this form makes a fine cut flower for the house. A variegated form of *A. major* has startling leaves splashed with cream, but it is still a rather rare plant and accordingly somewhat expensive. The pink flushed flowers of *A. maxima* are furnished with a deeper pink collar, and if one prefers even deeper colour there is *A. carniolica rubra* with deep red flowers on 18in stems, but neither of these have the full charm of the plainer relative. All the astrantias make dense clumps within a season and it is unusual not to find a few seedlings growing near the parent plant.

By contrast the growth rate of *Bupleurum angulosum* is slow but the small sprays of jade green flowers with neat pincushion centres are well worth waiting for. Some gardeners cosset this uncommon plant in special beds of greensand but providing it is given a fairly good soil that does not readily dry out and some shade, it will flower reliably every summer.

The roots of the trees and large shrubs which supply the required shade, can suck the ground bone dry, and when rain does come a great deal of it has to fall before such borders are properly soaked. Much can be done to minimise the water loss by mulches of dead leaves, coarse peat or any other bulky organic material that does not detract from the beauty of the border. The use of suitable plants, preferably with ground covering habits to keep what sun there may be off the soil will also help to conserve moisture ensuring a cool root run for as long as possible.

Epimediums will carry on unperturbed in dust dry soil and heavy shade. They have the wiry stems and leathery leaves that look as if they would survive under any conditions and the thick knotted root system is so congested as to be thoroughly weed proof. All the varieties have beautiful leaves, many of them evergreen and if the old leaves and stems are removed just as the new ones are beginning to appear at ground level, twelve months of immaculate ground cover can be relied on.

Two related plants, Solomon's Seal and *Smilacina racemosa* usually associated with cool moist soils are good at the back of a border under trees. The more common Solomon's Seal is still the most beautiful of the two with its arching stems spangled with broad leaves and clusters of green and white bells. The flowers of *Smilacina racemosa* would be more effective were they not such an indeterminate off-white, but their form, which is that of a large fluffy spike, is striking enough when seen against the fresh green leaves.

The leaves of the comfreys are bold and handsome enough if a trifle coarse when viewed against more delicate foliage. For this reason they are best kept at the back of the border where the tubular flowers can be seen to advantage early in the season and the large basal leaves left to provide ground cover later in the year. These again are inveterate seeders but are not difficult to remove.

Cultivated forms of our native woodruff are naturally at home under the dense shade of trees, their thready roots will run just below the surface of the soil sending up rosettes of bright green leaves, surmounted by heads of pure white flowers. In spite of its rapid progress it is a delicate plant that will not smother or harm anything but the smallest plants, most of which are in the alpine category and planted in more open conditions. There are some plants noted for their foliage that will only look their best in shade. In sun they either do not develop their finest colouring or the leaves are harmed by the first hot spell of sun. Many of these are golden leaved plants and are good for brightening shady borders. Mr Bowle's Golden Grass seeds itself in the right places once established, and from early spring until well after midsummer has leaves of the brightest gamboge yellow. A rare but easy plant with beautiful leaves is the golden form of meadowsweet, *Filipendula ulmaria aurea.* This plant insists on some shade and should be grown for the foliage alone. The flowers are pleasant and fragrant but add nothing to the general beauty of the plant.

If these are cut as soon as buds begin to show it will retain its character as a fine foliage plant until the end of the growing season.

The bold divided leaves of *Podophyllum emodi* with its apple blossom flowers and large seed capsules is an intriguing plant to grow in moist shade. Pale pink flowers on smooth stems rise out of the bare earth to be followed by the folded leaves, which burst through like mottled bronze umbrellas. In late summer and early autumn the flowers' stems bear large pendant crimson fruits which are said to be edible.

The brightly coloured allum root or heuchera is one of those pleasant little plants that flower unfailingly year after year seemingly without ever needing any but the most cursory attention. Best of all forms of this variable plant are probably the Bressingham hybrids with a wide range of shades, from pink to crimson and scarlet and when in flower in early summer they create a delightful haze of colour. With their rounded evergreen leaves they are doubly valuable and are, quite rightly, planted generously in many gardens.

Some of their near relations, all of the saxifrage family, while not having the intense colour of the hybrids are valuable and interesting plants and just as easy and trouble-free especially in light shade.

The most diminutive *Mitella brewerii* is an extremely neat plant with fresh green leaves that hug the ground and gradually spread to make good cover. It is an ideal plant for moist shady corners and sends up 3in spikes of minute green flowers with seed vessels that open like upturned cups.

Only a little larger but much more spectacular *Tiarella cordifolia* the foam flower thrives in the same sort of conditions. The well marked heart-shaped leaves are dense enough to subdue most weeds but are open enough to allow an underplanting of small bulbs. When established this plant will form wide mats and will be covered in spring by a foam of dainty fluffy heads of white flowers.

While by no means regarded as rampageous once established both these plants will quickly cover a sizable area with ground-hugging leaves.

The largest member of the family is *Tellima grandiflora* and this will do well in sun or shade. It is worth growing for the well marked and deeply veined hairy leaves alone. There is also a form listed as *T. grandiflora purpurea* whose leaves turn to shades of bronze and purple in the winter and are a good contrast to some of the winter flowering bulbs and green or cream hellebores. Small green bells, fringed with pink adorn the many 2ft spikes which this plant throws up. After flowering these are best removed immediately so that the full beauty of the leaves can be enjoyed once more.

The Pick-a-Back plant, *Tolmiea menziesii,* has been found to be perfectly hardy in most gardens and even remains reasonably evergreen. The chief attraction of this plant is its viviparous leaves. These are light green and rounded and produce young plants at the point where the leaf is joined to the stalk.

These can be detached and grown to make new clumps; if planted outdoors nature does this work for us as the leaves usually root wherever they touch the soil. With flowers rather like the heucheras but in shades of chocolate and green, they do need the right sort of background to be appreciated.

꙳꙳꙳꙳꙳꙳꙳꙳

Ferns

There are few gardeners who view the hardy ferns dispassionately.
The tendency has been to look on them as Victorian horrors to
be associated with overgrown laurels and dank grottos, and for
many years they have been neglected. There now seems to be a
revival of interest in ferns for the modern garden since their value
as a foliage plant has been realised. Many kinds will grow well in
the open border providing they are given a soil that does not dry
out too quickly. Although most species are essentially woodland
plants thriving in moist leafy soil, direct sunlight on the leaves
is by no means fatal.

In cool, shaded positions magnificent fronds are produced
with bright green leaves that fit in admirably with such broad-
leaved things as hostas and bergenias which also prefer these
surroundings. The evergreen kinds are invaluable for all-the-
year-round interest but in a mild locality many that are listed as
deciduous may well keep their leaves in a not too severe winter.

Of the evergreens, *Blechnum tabulare*, handsome as it is, is
only really suitable for mild districts but the refined fronds of the
polystichums, particularly *P. angulare*, keep their good looks no
matter how severe the weather. These tough ferns with decep-
tively delicate looking foliage have lacy fronds that lie horizontally in symmetrical rosettes 2ft across.

In the west country where it is plentiful, people tend to be
blasé about the native *Polypodium vulgare*, the Adders Fern; but
this should not be despised as a garden plant, for with its growing
habit and creeping rhizomatic roots it will make a solid and attractive ground cover for any shady spot. The smooth leathery fronds
always have a neat appearance, as do its improved forms *P.
macrostachyon* and *P. pulcherrimum*, luxuriant plants with lighter
green fronds. They are as hardy as the more common form.

The Harts Tongue fern is as well known as it is easy to grow, thriving in any shady corner or crevice. The strap-shaped fronds have gentle undulations as they uncurl from a central rosette and are perfect subjects for a quiet setting. The variety *Phyllitis undulatum* has beautiful exaggerated wavy edges but in appearance does not seem to be so much at home in the garden as in the green house. Where space permits, the Royal Fern, *Osmunda regalis,* can be planted. This deciduous plant is the largest of the hardy ferns and when grown in the right conditions is a magnificent sight. The young fronds unfurl a coppery brown.

For elegance of habit the slender Ostrich Fern can hardly be bettered although its upright habit does not make it the best of ground cover. This shuttlecock-shaped fern must have plenty of moisture, but when growing happily in a suitable soil it will spread and produce young plants from underground roots. Given a few inches of good soil with decaying leaves and vegetable matter, most ferns are tolerant of all conditions including chalk and once established should be trouble-free for many years.

Waterside Plants

In the shady garden, water is one of the more desirable elements whether it is in the form of pond or stream and if these are natural features so much the better for the general atmosphere of the garden. For the lucky few who have large ponds or broad streams, planting can be on the grand scale using some of the larger moisture-loving plants to good effect. Leaves that are 6ft across can only find a home in the larger garden yet this is the scale to which *Gunnera manicata* will grow when planted by water. It is a plant that never fails to fascinate by its sheer size, with great bottle brush flowers which break out of the coarse root-crowns at an early stage. Although quite hardy when established, it is susceptible to damage by frost and a covering of bracken over the crown will see it safely through the winter.

The arum flowers of the skunk cabbage are the showiest of all the early waterside spring flowers, rising out of the ground in yellow and white. The huge 4ft paddle-shaped leaves which follow are a good deep green and will smother any weeds at the water's edge.

For large plantings, the luxuriant leaves of the rodgersias are invaluable. Imposing 3ft stems uncurl crozier-like, topped with heads of pink and white fluffy flowers which are held well above a platform of leaves. The leaves of these plants vary in shape from the jagged lobes of *R. podophylla* to the great circular plates of *R. tabularis* and all have great architectural value. As weed suppressors at the waterside they have no equal and contrast beautifully with the sword shaped leaves of the irises and grasses that also prefer these conditions.

On a smaller scale the umbrella plant *Peltiphyllum peltatum* bears its starry pink flowers before the large rounded leaves unfold. This is a creeping rhizomatic plant with roots rather like an elephant's trunk which lie on the top of the ground, and is ideally suited to the edge of a small stream where it will help bind the soil together. There is no lack of plants to give spring colour in these conditions. Primulas and irises alone could give a glittering display for many weeks. Small plants of *Iris sibirica* soon thicken up into solid weed-proof bands of grassy leaves topped with clear blue or mauve flowers. The larger and more sumptuous irises, *I. kaempferi* and *I. laevigata* carry the season on into summer and are a little more demanding in moisture and a liking for lime-free soil.

The primulas that grow best at the water's edge are the tall ones, the candelabra varieties, including *P. japonica* and *P. pulverenta*, will provide all the pink and purple shades and the golden yellow flowers of *P. helodoxa* are a wonderful contrast to these.

Waterside flowers in the late summer are not so easy to come by but if one likes strong effects the larger senecios can be used. They are now usually listed under *ligularia*; the variety *clivorum* and its cultivar Desdemona are both bold plants with huge savage orange-coloured daisies that are superb for large plantings. The shaggy orange heads of *Ligularia Desdemona* can give a brilliant effect; for full impact they should be planted in broad masses. In spite of the glowing colour of its flowers and handsome deep green leaves with crimson reverses, this is a large somewhat coarse plant, best viewed from a distance for full effect. First coming into bloom in July its massed flower heads will develop into a sheet of orange keeping its good looks well into August. As a waterside plant it will tolerate some shade from surrounding trees but this should not be too deep or continuous.

With many fine cultivars and forms available, the colourful astilbe is fast becoming one of our favourite border flowers. They are, however, a species that require constant moisture if they are to give good heads of bloom and fresh foliage; ideally they should be grown at the waterside or in the bog garden.

Most of the medium-sized cultivars with their arching plumes of foaming flowers are never better than when planted in mass. The clumps of ferny foliage make splendid ground cover, taking on coppery tints in the spring when the young leaves unfurl. Some of the earlier flowering types are apt to have their foliage cut down by late frosts but usually recover well. The later flowering hybrids are much hardier and since all the astilbes seem to prefer semi-shade some protection can usually be arranged from adjacent shrubs.

The colour of the leaves and flowers is also undoubtedly better when protected from full sun. The leaves remain a fresh green and the flowers, particularly the crimsons and magentas, take on finer tones. For shady corners of the rockery there are some dwarf cultivars compact enough to grow alongside more delicate plants without harm. The white or pink-flowered *A. simplicifolia* has good glossy leaves to set off its fluffy spikes; while the raspberry-coloured *A. chinensis pumila* is an invaluable late flowerer.

One tall cultivar that invariably arouses admiration is the stately *A. taquetii superba*. It has such good form that it can stand alone as a specimen plant. The 4ft spikes are thickly encrusted with flowers between rose and deep magenta in late summer.

Climbing Plants

The various varieties of clematis must be the most popular and showy climbers in general use in our gardens, with different cultivars flowering over many months. For short bursts of spectacular colour these are justly prized and will embellish rather than smother any wall; but for the more adventurous gardener there are many climbers with fine leaves and fascinating flowers well worth growing for their unusual shape and colour.

Most climbing plants offered for sale in this country are strong doers and once started into growth will quickly cover their allotted space. The slender evergreen akebia with vigorous twining stems is not often seen. The variety *A. quinata* is the one usually grown with deep green fine-lobed leaves and drooping racemes of chocolate-purple flowers. The fruits which follow are sausage shaped and of a curious grey-violet which if sown in pots germinate with ease.

Another climber with flowers of even stranger shape is the Dutchman's pipe, *Aristolochia sipho*. This is also a lovely foliage plant worth growing for its large heart-shaped leaves alone which have the texture of velvet. This climbing birthwort is most attractive and does well on a wall of any aspect.

Bold heart-shaped leaves are also a feature of the actinidias. In *A. chinensis,* the Chinese gooseberry, these are set off against red hairy stems and since they are of large and impressive proportions they are worthy of an important site. A remarkable variety of this plant is *A. kolomikta* with tri-coloured variegation of green, white and pink. This variegation is best when the plants are situated against a south or west wall where they can benefit from full sun.

Enormous shield-shaped leaves are the main feature of *Vitis coignetiae*. These are beautifully veined and depending on the soil give a good show of autumn colour.

For simple bright colours from climbers the tropaeolums are worth a place where they can clamber among other shrubs and climbers. The half hardy canary creeper *T. peregrinum* has most attractive deeply-lobed light green leaves and the small but showy lemon yellow flowers are good for the whole summer. In England, *T. speciosum*, the flame nasturtium usually proves to be rather difficult but in Scotland it romps away creeping through and decorating neighbouring shrubs. While this nasturtium is perennial the top growth will be completely killed off most winters but usually re-appears again in spring poking through the ground in unexpected places.

Page 105   17 *One of the most striking of all the geraniums,* G. psilostemon, *forms a huge clump of deeply cut leaves surmounted by magenta flowers with black centres*

18 *The herbaceous* Clematis integrifolia *is a graceful plant with purple-blue flowers that can be left to sprawl or persuaded to climb into small shrubs*

Page 106   19 *Only in the wild garden can the enormous* Heracleum mantegazzianum *be allowed to seed*
20 *Of the ornamental rhubarbs the red leaved forms are most effective.* Rheum palmatum *grows to eight feet and requires moist soil*

4

Roses

Today the rose garden proper is not fashionable. In these days of smaller gardens it takes up too much space and has little to offer for six months of the year. The modern trend is for roses of all kinds to be grown in conjunction with shrubs and border plants, attractive to look at but making the business of care and upkeep all the more difficult and scratchy.

The vogue for growing shrub roses, especially as a background to the mixed border, is one of the more satisfactory ways of giving an air of maturity to a planting. There is now an immense range of roses from which to make a choice—species, old roses and the comparatively more recent hybrid perpetuals, hybrid musks, bourbons and modern shrub roses.

There is a tendency to deplore the lack of fragrance in most of the modern roses; for anyone who has grown the old roses, there is nothing to surpass their fragrance in a midsummer garden with scents that are detected by the nose long before the eye beholds the bloom. Fragrance that will carry is valuable in any garden, and many of the tall scented shrub roses which usually stand well back in the border have this characteristic.

Hybrid musks in particular will throw their pungent scent for yards, the varieties Cornelia, Felicia and Pax being intense enough to compete with that other deliciously scented June shrub, the philadelphus.

Pruning and controlling some of the more exuberant shrub roses can be something of a problem especially when the plants are beginning to mature and make vigorous growth annually. The robust self-standing forms with strong stems are no problem at all and there are many that may be left unpruned except for shaping and the removal of dead and weak growth.

Stem Support

Others like the hybrid musk Moonlight or the modern hybrid shrub rose Constance Spry send out long stems that are so lax that the great weight of midsummer bloom bears the branches to the ground. Without some form of support these vigorous roses can look appalling after summer winds or rain. Single stakes, however stout, are not the answer. Tying in a large shrub that depends on the natural grace of its arching branches for effect can never be successful and will certainly do nothing to help the growth of the plant.

As with other plants the simplest and most natural methods of support are usually the best and if one can utilise natural features of the garden this is far preferable to introducing some foreign element. Support and accommodation for the larger shrub roses and climbers can be arranged by training the shoots into nearby trees and shrubs. Once established on the host plant maintenance is relatively simple.

One of the most effective ways in which I have seen this problem tackled with medium-sized shrub roses is by using a triangle of sheep hurdles to encase a luxuriant specimen of Constance Spry. This rose is notorious for its heavy masses of bloom at midsummer, which can be completely ruined by a summer storm unless adequate support is given. Old gates and post and rail fences in fact, make ideal supports and look so much more natural than contrived supports, however sophisticated they may be.

Another way of dealing with roses of this habit is to peg down the arching stems either directly into the ground or to tie them along the length of arching hazel wands which are secured to the ground at either end. This method should ensure a more or less even amount of growth along the whole of the stem but unless one can be absolutely sure that the ground beneath them is clear of perennial weeds, cleaning the soil in subsequent seasons will be extremely painful if not impossible. Some of these sprawlers, like *R. macrantha raubritter* whose habit is ideal for this treatment, are extremely prickly.

Old Roses

In spite of the drawback of having only one season of bloom no gardener who loves good plants can afford to ignore the old roses which are at their best at midsummer. With their globular, cabbage or quartered blooms they are the romantics of the garden, with such memorable and beautiful names that alone justify them a place. Most of them were Victorian favourites and are now firmly established back in fashion and receiving the attention they deserve after many years of neglect. A preponderance of these have names of a French flavour and historic associations, such as Chapeau de Napoleon, the crested moss or Cardinal de Richelieu, a sumptous maroon gallica. Even the names of the groups to which these roses belong conjure up the image of character and elegance and, coupled with the fragrance with which most of them are well endowed, they are irresistible to those gardeners who are not of the hybrid tea persuasion.

Of the vigorous alba group *Alba maxima*, the double white Jacobite rose, is a shrub that will reach 6ft in height and 5ft across, and at midsummer is covered with ivory blooms to be followed later by oval hips. Two fine pink varieties, Celeste and Maiden's Blush, are typical of the group with grey-green leaves which are a perfect background to the soft pink flowers.

The centifolias include the old cabbage rose or Provençe Rose and Chapeau de Napoleon with its clear pink blooms and a prominent cockade of moss encasing the buds. Though rather lax and open in habit, they are good roses especially in the mixed border where the base of the plants can be masked by foliage. As developments of the centifolias, the moss roses have great appeal; the moss covered buds playing no small part in the beauty and interest of the plant. The exquisite quartered blooms with green pointels of such varieties as Marechal Davoust and Gloire des Mousseux are the highlight of the season. The foliage and moss of the latter plant is a most beautiful clear light green, setting off extremely large clean pink double flowers that can be as much as 5in across.

A rose of great interest but perhaps not showy enough for the small garden is the York and Lancaster rose, *R. damascena versicolour*. This has some blooms of pink some of white and others with parti-coloured petals. Needing a strong and rich soil if it is to give of its best, this ancient rose is supposedly the one which supplied the symbols to the opposing factions in the Wars of the Roses. In this group the pink Celsiana is a more vigorous plant for the garden with masses of semi-double flowers and grey foliage. The autumn damask, Quatre Saisons is yet another rose of great antiquity going back to pre-Roman times, but again is of more historic interest than garden value. Its mossy sport has poorish flowers, but the group is redeemed by such good garden varieties as Marie Louise, Mme Zoetmans, Ispahan and Leda, the painted damask with white petals edged with crimson.

For a touch of gaiety and flamboyance, some of the gallica roses, especially those with stripes and splashes on their petals are invaluable in the June garden. Most plants in this group are neat and shapely shrubs and include the old crimson *R. officinalis* and its offspring Rosa Mundi, probably the most telling of all roses when covered with its crimson and white striped flowers and bosses of golden stamens.

These lovely plants with their subtle colourings, ranging through mauve, purple, pink, crimson and white, are most effective when grown away from the more modern kinds especially if they have warm or hot colouring. They are best associated with underplanting of good foliage—sages, lavenders and hardy geraniums are ideal. The colourings will never clash and the leaves are rarely damaged by the thorny stems.

Shrub Roses

Some of the Victorian shrub roses with strong growing habits like the hybrid perpetuals and the more recent hybrid musks can be relied on to give a tremendous display. In June and July these shrubs are heavily laden with a mass of small to medium sized blooms and in late summer give a second burst of flowers that continue until late in the year. The named varieties Felicia, Buff Beauty, and Cornelia are particularly good in the garden and as cut flowers. When the first frosts begin unopened buds can be brought indoors. The small hard terra-cotta buds of Cornelia are best of all for this purpose and open to an intense coppery pink far removed from the paler shades of early summer.

The tall-growing Moonlight is another that can give huge

autumn trusses of small white flowers embossed with golden stamens. This particular plant can climb 10ft or so and has good dark green foliage on plum coloured stems. The unfortunately named Magenta ends its season with a magnificent final burst, usually in late October. Sometimes listed as a floribunda shrub rose, this has some of the finest flowers of all being of soft lilac purple suffused with pink and deserving a far more sympathetic title to describe its merits. The pronounced musky fragrance of *Rosa moschata,* one of the parents of these hybrids has been perpetuated in many of the named forms while Buff Beauty exhales a strong tea scent and others have their own intense fragrance.

The Bourbons if not quite so exuberant offer exquisite shapely blooms. This is particularly true of the elegant Louise Odier and Mme Pierre Oger, whose bowl-shaped flowers have such perfection of form and neatness of habit. Late blooms rarely seem to be malformed by light frosts and retain their perfect form for several days. In the same group the slender La Reine Victoria is noted for its generous display of flowers. These have the same globular shape, the outer petals forming a perfect circle enclosing a mass of shell-like petals.

That superb rose Mme Isaac Pereire is the most vigorous of all the bourbons with handsome foliage to set off its enormous flowers. These are quartered and very full, of deep dusky pink and with a rich fragrance. This great rose can be used as a self-standing shrub or used to cover a wall or pillar or allowed to grow naturally into a hedge.

The claim could be made for that odd but beautiful little rose Stanwell Perpetual that it is usually the first to flower and the last to shed its blooms. This is a delightful little shrub with arching thorny stems and delicate grey-green leaves. Like many of the old roses it begins its season with a smother of soft pink flowers that fade to white in hot weather. The folded petals eventually open flat revealing a muddled centre. After its first mid summer flowering this shrub is rarely without some flowers to decorate its lax stems.

Of the modern shrub roses, all of them fine plants, there are a few that are outstanding, having the informal character of the old roses and the recurrent flowering qualities of the modern hybrids.

Now almost universally classed as a shrub rose, Queen Elizabeth with its upright growth and clusters of clear pink flowers is probably best known for its continuous flowering. The lax growth of Constance Spry, another pink rose with large centifolia-type flowers need some support in the form of a hedge or fence. It is however one of the most charming of all modern roses when in full bloom in June and July, and is accompanied by a rich fragrance.

The largest of this group is Nevada and grown as a free standing shrub it will reach a height of 7ft with a corresponding width. The long arching stems of this rose make a dense thicket and when laden with hundreds of cream single blooms it is a super-lative sight. For another floriferous rose whose stems bow under the weight of bloom, Fritz Nobis is incomparable. Shapely buds open into soft pink flowers with deeper shadings above dense mid-green leaves. This is another rose whose clove fragrance has been retained.

The large, almost single blooms of Erfurt shade to a broad pale zone around the golden stamens and are always in evidence during the growing season. This is a most satisfactory medium-sized rose with burnished leaves and a rich scent. There are few yellows among the shrub roses but Golden Moss and Golden Wings are two of the best. The former has deep green leaves and dark moss from which the double flowers open, pale yellow with deeper tones at the centre.

Golden Wings is a later addition and is a perpetual flowering rose with large single yellow flowers set on russet stems. This is another compact rose suitable for the small border.

᪥᪥᪥᪥᪥᪥᪥᪥

Rugosa Roses

The rugosa roses are an extremely hardy group from north-east Asia that will tolerate the coldest conditions and begin to flower at the end of May and continue through until early autumn. For those who garden on sandy soils this is a good rose and ideal for maritime districts. While it is not recommended for clay or chalk, plants growing in these soils seem to thrive well enough. Mildew, blackspot and other leaf diseases common to the rose rarely affect the deeply veined and glossy rugosa foliage, while the infestation of pests is hardly noticeable. The typical and less hybridised forms of *Rosa rugosa* are wonderful garden shrubs making well-rounded dense plants noted for flowers and hips, the foliage turning to a rich butter yellow in autumn. In some forms particularly Frau Dagmar Hastrup and Scabrosa, the huge hips an inch or more wide hang like crimson tomatoes and coincide with the late summer burst of bloom. The most beautiful of all, the semi-double Roseraie de L'Hay has no hips but loses nothing in effect by their absence. From elegant scrolled and pointed buds emerge a succession of rich, crimson-purple flowers with loosely folded petals of velvet texture. This is a truly perpetual rose, early flowering and building up over the years into a shrub exceeding 5ft in height and width.

Like most of the shrub roses little pruning except for shaping is necessary, although some cutting back of shoots will ensure an even greater show of flowers.

One of the few disadvantages of this beautiful group is the excessive prickliness of the stems. These are literally covered with small spines and bristles which do not help the plants reputation as a cut flower but add immensely to the effectiveness of the shrubs when grown as a hedge. After a very few years most forms become solid enough to make formidable barriers that can be kept in shape by clipping as a form of pruning. White forms are especially good when grown in association with Roseraie de L'Hay. The best of these is the pure-white Blanc double de Coubert with semi-double flowers of a crinkled and papery quality and more lax in habit than most of the others. The single white form Alba, has a well clothed and bushy habit and sports a fine crop of orange hips in late summer, again coinciding with the second main show of bloom.

A tall hybrid that is very near to *R. rugosa* in growth and habit and should be more widely grown is the floriferous silver pink Sarah Van Fleet. This is a rose of erect growth with superb bronze tinted leaves and will quickly reach 8ft. Flowering freely the whole summer with large heads of bloom it will continue as one of the brightest shrubs in the garden until early autumn. The typical rich clove scent of the rugosa varies in strength from rose to rose but is particularly pronounced in Sarah Van Fleet and Roseraie de L'Hay.

Climbing Roses

Walls and fences to provide support for climbing roses are not always readily available and most gardeners have to limit their choice to one or two varieties at the most. In such cases the choice is usually a conservative one of Albertine, Pauls Scarlet, American Pillar or Dorothy Perkins.

In June, these roses, some good and others rather coarse provide sheets of colour which are effective at a distance but their indiscriminate use does not always harmonise with the surroundings or stand up to close inspection.

Superb climbers or ramblers like Lady Hillingdon, Mme Gregoire Staechelin or Felicite et Perpetue are not now seen enough in gardens or catalogues. Unlike so many climbers that have only one flush of bloom the apricot coloured Lady Hillingdon is seldom without some flowers. The loose double flowers with their strong tea scent are set off against dark glossy foliage and are most useful as a mellowing influence against raw red brick.

Another vigorous yellow with recurring blooms that deserves to be planted more often is Lawrence Johnston. This climber which has been grown at Hidcote for many years was formerly known as Hidcote Yellow. It has perfect pointed buds opening to loose lemon yellow flowers which show up well against the rich mid-green foliage. This is a large and vigorous rose but the sister seedling Le Rêve, which is similar in all its parts, is more restrained in its rate of growth and only climbs to 15ft.

For best effect the climbing form of hybrid tea rose Mme Gregoire Staechelin needs a background of old stone to complement its trusses of large pink flowers. This is inclined to be an early flowering rose and is one of the taller climbers reaching up to 30ft. It is reputed to do well on a north wall.

The larger ramblers, especially the multifloras, never look better than when allowed to grow naturally and without restriction or into huge mounds. Gold Finch is one of the best of these giving a generous smother of fragrant yellow flowers fading to cream in hot sun. Almost thornless stems makes this a fairly harmless rose for a position near a path and if left unpruned will mound itself into a huge hummock of 10ft high and through. Another multiflora, Rambling Rector, is so thorny and wilful as to defy pruning. At midsummer when in full bloom this rose is an amazing sight with a foam of thousands of small white flowers and a far carrying fragrance.

Another such rambler is the fragrant Francis E. Lester that will climb into trees for 15ft or so and make a dense shrub covered with apple-blossom-like flowers.

Roses like this, that will go on happily for years with little or no pruning will eventually mound up into wide bushes. Even the relatively small Felicite et Perpetue, one of the hardiest of all ramblers, is best trained upwards and then allowed to cascade, forming a continually thickening mound. When covered with its white rosette flowers and carmine buds this is one of the most charming of all summer sights.

Rose Hedges

Some of the bolder shrub roses and climbers can also be used to form or thicken up boundary hedges while the smaller compact roses like the Gallicas and Rugosas make excellent dividing hedges. Modern hybrids, teas and floribundas are quite useless for this purpose although a number of the modern shrub roses like Fritz Nobis and Nevada are vigorous enough and have the right bushy habit.

For a boundary hedge where space and formality is not important, magnificent effects can be obtained by using some of the larger species that make dense thickets of thorny branches. Both the white *R. multiflora* and the yellow *R. cantabrigensis* have vigorous growth and a good bushy habit with no gaps at the base. The ferny foliage of the latter is attractive throughout the growing season and might well be planted alongside the even larger *R. Highdownensis* which has similar lacy leaves and single crimson blooms. Some of the taller-growing shrub roses are often recommended for use as hedges and while they will give a long season of colour and grow tall enough to screen most gardens they are usually rather thin at the base and need thickening up with a supplementary planting of low growing shrubs. These are good where space is too limited for the stronger growing species. For the smaller gardens roses trained on wires stretched between stout poles will take up far less width and allow for easier training. Roses with strong arching shoots like *R. complicata, R. Paulii,*

Mme Isaac Periere or many of the exquisite Fruhlings group lend themselves to this form of training with comparative ease.

Inevitably such a screen or hedge may look rather thin in the winter months when the leaves have fallen, but the inclusion of one or two varieties that hold their leaves longer than most will help to keep the screen furnished. The leaves of the thornless Bourbon climber Zephirine Drouhin are particularly tenacious; and while the popular climber Mermaid is suspect as to hardiness in a really cold winter, the leaves are mostly evergreen and of good texture and colour. The perpetual flowering habit and fragrance of this rose make it an especially valuable addition in such a setting. Whether grown as screens or hedges the taller roses are splendid hosts to the less vigorous clematis. Those that annually produce a mass of foliage should be avoided but delicate varieties like the viticella group will extend the period of interest for many weeks.

Where supports are not possible, tall self-standing shrubs might well be used without taking up too much space at ground level. With a minimum of pruning and an occasional tying in, the hybrid musks are superb for this purpose. There are at least a dozen of this family that will quickly make a 6ft hedge with perpetual or recurrent flowers and all with great personality, and a fragrance that carries for yards. Some of the rugosa roses and their hybrids are possibly the best of all roses for hedge-making. Being endowed with ample thorns and bristles they make a good protective barrier clothed with crinkled shiny leaves typical of all the rugosas.

Sarah van Fleet with its free flowering habit and erect growth is one of the best for a self-supporting 6ft hedge. This rugosa has a long season of bloom with masses of silvery pink flowers from late spring until autumn. The other tall rugosa often recommended is Schneezwerg, a neat but vigorous shrub with small leaves and a continuous display of white flowers followed by small orange hips. On a slightly smaller scale the rugosas Frau Dagmar

Hastrup and Scabrosa with pink and magenta flowers respectively and the sumptuous velvety purple Roseraie de L'Hay make magnificent dividing hedges within a garden. The fruits of the first two which coincide with the late summer blooms are strong in colour and add to the late summer scene. Rugosas treated as hedges are fairly carefree shrubs and can be kept compact and shapely by a late winter clipping with shears and the tying in of long shoots later in the season. That group of roses known as the Old Roses are also amenable to this sort of treatment and make extremely showy hedges of medium height. The gallicas Belle de Crecy, *R. officinalis* and the striped Rosa Mundi are all good where one requires the cool mauves and crimsons so essential to the mature garden.

5

Late Summer

Cutting Back

By late summer most borders assume the tired and blowsy look of plants left to their own devices after the flowering period. Such a sight can be almost as distressing as that of a weed infested garden but with a little care and determination to use the knife wherever needed, borders need not look like a jungle.

With so many plants a second crop of flowers comes as a bonus if old stems are removed as soon as the first flush of bloom is over and go some way to preventing unsightly gaps in the late season.

The term dead-heading is unfortunately taken literally by too many gardeners. If one indulges in the tedious business of removing individual heads, this job can be the chore it sounds. There is little point in snipping away at solitary blooms if the end result is a mass of headless stems that will eventually die back. A certain amount of ruthlessness is called for with some of

120

the more exuberant plants and taking the shears to them rather than the knife can do nothing but good. Some of the hardy geraniums such as *G. endressii, G. punctatum* and *G. Claridge Druce* are particularly responsive to this treatment. After the first showing of flowers, the long leafy stems are inclined to straggle and become tatty. If the top growth is sheared away, fresh green foliage and masses of new bloom will quickly reappear.

Lamiums, feverfews, mints and some of the smaller creeping decorative grasses can be treated this way. Even some of the species and rugosa roses will benefit from an occasional clipping especially when grown as hedges. Hedges of Rosa Mundi can be kept compact and lose nothing of their glorious mid-summer display. The rugosas will repay amply for an early clipping by giving masses of bloom throughout the season.

Other tall plants, like delphiniums and *Campanula persicifolia,* can usually be induced to send up further spikes of bloom if the spent ones are removed immediately after flowering. These are rarely as large and imposing as the midsummer spikes but add a welcome note of colour in the later months. The silver foliaged santolinas and blue-leaved rues are shrubs that need cutting back hard in early spring for the best display of fresh foliage. An occasional clipping in the summer will not come amiss to prevent the new growth from becoming too leggy. Beautiful as these plants are in full leaf they will suffer in winter if the new growth is not shortened. Both are valuable evergreens but a moderate fall of snow can quickly break off whole portions of a plant if it is not compact enough to withstand the weight.

The vast range of plants that are too generous with seedlings can be dealt with while the shears are out. Some inveterate seeders with long tap roots such as fennel and the symphytums can be troublesome if the seeds are allowed to ripen and should be cut as soon as the flowers have faded. The fennel, especially the purple leaved form, is far too good a foliage plant to cut to the ground. If the stems are simply shortened to prevent flowering the result will be a much bushier plant that will stand in the border like a column of smoke.

❦❦❦❦❦❦❦❦

Late Flowering and Foliage

Plants with daisy-like flowers in the late summer border are on the whole a dull lot when not in bloom and have little to offer in the way of good foliage to justify important positions in the garden. There are a few exceptions like celmisia and anthemis, both of which have magnificent grey leaves that are far superior in quality to their quite ordinary white daisy flowers. At the other end of the scale the shasta daisies, while delightful in the shaggy magnificence of their flowers, have leaves that can only be described as dead green. Since this plant and its cultivars make robust clumps it will need careful placing in the middle of the border if its leaves are not to become a dominating mass.

For a greater variety of colourful daisy flowers in the summer months the erigerons will begin to put on a dazzling show in June.

When properly grown, these neat daisies are capable of flowering on until September in compact mounds that will need little attention. Blue, pink and mauve are the predominant colours. The early flowering white form Simplex is the dwarf of the family, barely reaching a foot in height compared with the 18in violet Dignity or the 2ft pink Gaiety.

Stokes' aster has the accommodating habit of furnishing the garden throughout the year with a rosette of evergreen basal leaves. Early in August the plant is studded with 3in wide flowers of lavender blue set on branching stems. There are a number of good forms available of *Stoksia laevis* which is itself a variable plant, Blue Star being one of the best, having the cleanest colours and the largest flowers.

Page 123   21 *For the*
back of the border the
biennial onopordons make
a lattice of silver grey

22 *The best eryngium for*
bold effect is the biennial
E. giganteum *with soft*
blue flowers and glaucous
collars

24 *The Ostrich fern,*
Matteuccia struthiopteris, *makes a shuttlecock of delicate leaves each spring*

Page 124   23 *The variegated astrantia is a magnificent foliage plant with its cream and yellow markings*

25 *The variegated form of* Brunnera macrophylla *is an uncommon plant. Sprays of bright blue flowers contrast with the showy leaves*

Another daisy with indifferent foliage that can be excused on account of its magnificent flowers is the dimorphotheca, the African daisy, with its various forms. These need and deserve a warm and sheltered position in full sun as the flowers will not open in shade or in dull weather. The orange forms of *D. aurantiaca* are extremely showy plants, but it is the curiously luminous quality of *D. barberiae* and *D. ecklonis* that make them such useful plants in the border where a light note is required. The aristocrat of this pair is *D. ecklonis* with brilliant white petals surrounding a violet zone. In a well-drained sheltered position, it will usually survive our winters but is not reliably hardy. For this reason a few young plants which are easily struck from cuttings should be overwintered in a cold frame to ensure a succession of plants the following season. A prostrate form of this species that is just as hardy and floriferous is a valuable plant where space in favoured spots is limited. The pink flowered *D. barberiae* is said to be perfectly hardy and for a daisy has fairly good evergreen aromatic foliage. Although the dimorphothecas are not long lived plants especially on cold clay soils, they will in time make big clumps covering several square feet of soil. At this stage they tend to sprawl and should be cut back hard in spring. This will give a more shapely clump and rejuvenated foliage although the flowering period will be delayed by a few weeks. The less exuberant form *D. barberiae compacta* is a good choice for the small garden although while quite hardy its foliage disappears during the winter.

The popular Michaelmas daisies also have some of the least interesting leaves of all border plants and one has to either mask their lanky growth with more attractive foliage or put up with it for a long time until the flowers appear in the autumn. The hybrid *Aster x frikartii* is a notable exception and while its grey green leaves are not dense enough to indicate any planned form, the flowers do begin their display in July and carry on through to October. The intense lavender blue of the petals surrounding a yellow disc is one of the cleanest and most satisfactory of colours for the summer border.

Among the many forms of late summer and autumn flowering aster the small flowered specimens are seldom seen. When compared with their stiff stemmed relatives, the Michaelmas daisies, they are undeniably less colourful; but what they lack in size of the individual flowers is amply compensated for by the number of minute blooms. At their peak they make a haze of soft colour which lasts for several weeks.

Species like *Aster cordifolius* or *A. corymbosus* are endowed with strong slender stems that are tough and wiry and require only the lightest twigging for support. The American wood aster, *A. cordifolius,* the taller of the two, is most useful when grown as a fill-in between early flowering plants or shrubs. It will tolerate some shade and by late summer its long stems will have reached their full height, gaining support from adjacent plants to give a cloud of small starry flowers on the multi-branched stems. The variety Silver Spray has flowers of pale lilac, while those of Ideal are of light blue. Both foliage and habit of these small flowered species is far superior to the hybrid Michaelmas daisies and the deep green broad leaves of *A. corymbosus* which are set on wiry black stems are most elegant of all. When topped with a mist of white flowers the colour combination is very good. This is one of the easiest of all asters to grow, thriving in sun or part shade and requiring no staking.

The flower mass of the *A. ericoides* varieties is so solid that it gives the effect of a dense and shapely bush. This is the White Heath Aster of Eastern America and Canada, whose leaves in all its forms are small and shaped like those of the heathers. This bushy species with widely branching heads has a broad colour range. Two good yellows are Brimstone and Golden Spray, while Ringdove has decided rosy tints to its lavender flowers. The best white form is Perfection; but it is not such an effective plant as the coloureds. This species will tolerate fairly dry soil conditions and as a cut flower will last for weeks.

The species of *A. linosyris* is usually represented by the variety Goldilocks, a plant with showers of button heads without rays. An improved form Gold Dust, although reaching some 30in in height, needs little staking since the willowy stems are tough and resilient. The weight of the flower mass on thin stems, however tough obviously creates some problems especially in wet weather and this should be considered when planting the more floriferous kinds. One species that always remains neat and upright whatever the weather is *A. diffusus horizontalis*. This stiff wide-spreading plant looks good from the time it makes its basal leaves in spring, until well into the autumn when its spent flower heads are rimed with frost.

Much of the merit of these small flowered species is their moderate rate of growth. While making substantial bushy plants with masses of flower, the root system does not ramp and frequent division is unnecessary. If the plants are to be increased the roots are easily teased apart and re-established after flowering or during the spring.

Sedums

Beginning their flowering display in August, a more reliable and easily pleased group of plants than the border sedums would be hard to find. Sun, ordinary soil and adequate drainage is all that is necessary for a good display; they are rarely troubled by disease or weather.

The ubiquitous *Sedum spectabile* more commonly known as the ice plant and so often frequented by butterflies is a splendid subject for any garden and remains a firm favourite in spite of the various improved forms that have appeared in nurserymen's lists over the last decade. These new cultivars have all the good qualities of *S. spectabile* but are improved in size and colour and associate well with the pale lavender blue of the asters and perovskia which also flower at this season. One of the larger ones, *S. spectabile,* Autumn Joy, with its rich green and bronze heads and glaucous foliage gives a warm and luxuriant effect to any border.

Sedum Meteor has much deeper coloured flowers while *S.* Brilliant is as its name implies a very showy plant forming dense clumps with flat pink heads. One of the smaller border sedums with very fine purple-grey leaves is a more recently introduced hybrid called Ruby Glow. Instead of the usually stiff erect stems this plant has a rather sprawling habit and sends out stems horizontally over the ground terminating in heads of dusky magenta flowers making a mat some 9in high.

The tallest sedum, *S. maximum atropurpureum,* has rich maroon colouring to its stems and leaves which are more striking than the heads of red flowers. Unfortunately, this is a rather sparse plant and does not thicken to make such a dense clump as the others but it is well worth growing for foliage alone, especially if contrasted against silver leaves or the blue foliage of rue or *Acaena ascendens.* The heavy stems of this plant will reach 2ft. Since it is of such open habit staking with a few twigs is advisable.

At the other end of the colour scale the one yellow sedum suitable for borders is *S. aizoon* which produces heads of butter yellow flowers in July amid bright green leaves. This old garden plant is not seen so often in gardens, but is of pleasing habit, and the stems and flower heads remain decorative throughout the winter, turning to a strong rust colour.

Interest is provided very early in the year when the rosettes begin to swell making domes of decorative foliage. It is at this stage that the variegated ice plant *Sedum albo roseum variegatum* is seen to advantage and the beautifully marked fleshy leaves may be admired to the full. The variegation is of cream on light green and can create a brilliant effect in full sun. The young foliage begins life in delicate shades of pink turning to green later in the year and losing much of its charm but with its pale pink heads it is still well worth a place at the front of autumn border.

$\overset{\scriptscriptstyle ?}{\text{℃}}\overset{\scriptscriptstyle ??}{\text{℃}}\overset{\scriptscriptstyle ??}{\text{℃}}\overset{\scriptscriptstyle ??}{\text{℃}}\overset{\scriptscriptstyle ??}{\text{℃}}\overset{\scriptscriptstyle ??}{\text{℃}}\overset{\scriptscriptstyle ?}{\text{℃}}$

Fuchsia

One of the easiest plants to grow must be the fuchsia. Stick any cutting into a pot of reasonable soil or even directly into the ground, and there is every chance that it will take and put on growth in the season. The hardy forms of this accommodating family can be depended on to flower right through the latter half of the summer and well into autumn.

The dozen or so hardies available although annually cut down by the frost in cold districts rarely fail to send up new shoots in the spring while in the extreme west of England and Ireland fuchsia hedges are seldom affected and will grow into large shrubs. While having smaller flowers than the tender varieties once the blooms begin, there is no off season and the spent flowers fall gracefully, making way for further blooms.

The various forms of *Fuchsia magellanica* are all hardy, *F. m. riccartonii* being particularly so, as well as being one of the most vigorous with its branching plum-coloured stems and crimson flowers. The variety *F. magellanica thompsonii* is a more slender plant with matt green leaves but the amount of flower produced in a season even in the shade is prodigous. Another splendid fuchsia which grows to the same height of about 3ft is Chilerton Beauty, a form with light pink sepals and lilac skirt.

Like many plants with pendulous flowers, fuchsias are most effective if they can be planted above eye level so that the full beauty of the sepals and the 'skirt' can be appreciated. In general habit the hardy fuchsias are best planted singly to show off the graceful outline of the plant. They are completely self-supporting and twigging or stakes should never be needed.

Dark green opposite leaves and arching stems of these hardy fuchsias assort well with other plants in the mixed border and the variegated form *F. gracilis tricolour* with cream and green leaves edged with pink is worth a special place with a dark background.

Fruits and Berries

It is inevitable at the end of the season that attention is centred on the wide range of colourful fruits and berries that come as a bonus after the summer flowers. Many of these are borne on trees and shrubs and last for a long time, some well into the winter.

There are many foliage and border plants that also give good berries and it is surprising that these are so often neglected. They do much to prolong the season of colour at ground level and, unlike the berries of many of the shrubs, birds tend to leave them alone.

Pride of place must go to species and shrub roses many of which have splendid hips. There are none larger or more showy than those of the rugosas, *R. rugosa scabrosa* and *R. rugosa* Frau Dagmar Hastrup. These are tomato shaped and well over an inch across. When fully ripened they usually coincide with the second main show of single flowers in late summer. The species roses that we value for their hips flower once only, usually at midsummer but the range of fruits produced is wide and varies in shape from the small round hips of *R. rubrifolia* and *R. cantabrigensis* to the large flagon-shaped fruits of *R. setipoda* and *R. moyesii*. All shades of orange, red, brown and maroon are represented, most of them shining and giving a brilliant display. These are of great value as background material in the autumn garden and will fit in well with shrubs at the back of the border.

It is at this time of the year that the berried spikes of Lords and Ladies are at their best. Even the common woodlander *Arum maculatum* is worth keeping under hedges and in out of the way places. The form with variegated leaves, *A. italicum pictum*, which emerges from the soil after the flower spikes, is much the best one to grow and increases satisfactorily in heavy soil. In such a situation it will produce stout stems encrusted with brilliant orange berries that are good for many weeks. This plant produces its fine leaves during the winter months when they can be fully appreciated. They are extremely tough and frost resistant and are ideal for underplanting among shrubs where their cream and white marbled leaves make distinctive ground cover.

The Chinese Lantern plant or Winter Cherry, *Physalis franchettii* is hardly a plant for refined borders but given ample space in the wilder part of the garden where it can spread unhindered it is capable of putting on a magnificent autumn show. This plant in its original form *P. alkekengi*, growing some 15in high, is an old cottage garden plant and seems to have been used extensively before the introduction of the improved Japanese form *P. franchettii*, a taller plant growing up to 30in with calyxes 2½in long. With such a rampageous plant, one might as well grow the largest and most magnificent form—*P. f. gigantea*, a stately plant that can put on a magnificent show when given its head with ample space.

Apart from fresh green heart-shaped leaves and tall stems the plant has little to offer until the autumn, the flower being insignificant in size and colour. In late summer the seed pods begin to take shape and are attractive in all their stages from soft green to brilliant orange. The papery lantern-shaped calyx which encloses the globular fruit is much tougher than one would imagine and is extremely persistent. Picked at their peak, they are easily dried for winter decoration. Although this is an undeniably invasive plant spreading by thick underground stolons, it does need a rich moist soil to give of its best and will put up with some shade. Should the plant spread too much, it can be contained by spading around the edges and lifting the unwanted roots which lie a few inches under the ground.

Actaea rubra, with ferny foliage and spikes of translucent crimson berries is a plant that always arouses interest. The foliage which makes excellent ground cover is pierced by stiff stems topped with clusters of berries and will thrive in light shade under trees and shrubs.

An evergreen iris which will grow in half shade is the Gladwin, *Iris foetidissima.* The flowers of this plant are beautiful but not particularly showy. The pods of orange seeds which follow and open up in the autumn are magnificent and show off well against the deep shining green leaves. The variegated form of this iris is a fine foliage plant but does not flower so freely as its plain counterpart.

One of the most fascinating plants in all seasons is *Podophyllum emodi* whose pale pink flowers appear before the leaves have developed. These push through the ground like bronze-green umbrellas to a height of 18in and in late summer and autumn are hung with pendant fruits. Another species of this family, *P. peltatum,* the American mandrake or May Apple has scarlet fruits which ripen as early as July, and being up to 2in long make a good show.

The pokeberry, *Phytolacca americana,* is a large, coarse, but striking border plant with spikes of inky black berries. The berries are set closely together and filled with a crimson juice which has led to its nickname of red ink plant. The odour of this plant is rather unpleasant and the seeds being poisonous it is best not to handle these. For indifferent soil and poor conditions, *Hypericum calycinum* is a well known stand-by. A bushier member of this family, *H. elatum* which becomes broad and dense with age has some of the handsomest berries of all. Far more showy than the flowers, the clusters of seed capsules, pointed and bright scarlet will in a good season cover the whole bush.

Autumn Bulbs

There are only a few bulbs that flower reliably in our gardens during the autumn but among these few the colchicums are the most spectacular of the small bulbs. Commonly called autumn crocuses, these bulbs are superficially much like the hybrid Dutch crocuses of spring with large open cups. Botanically there are wide differences between the two, the main ones affecting the gardener are the size of bulb and of the large leaves that appear in spring. These leaves can be a problem in the border since they are not particularly decorative and disproportionately large in relation to the flower, occupying space at a time when it is valuable.

They can be accommodated more easily in clumps in shrubberies or naturalised in rough grass together with daffodils and other spring flowering bulbs. This method is probably the most satisfactory since the leaves can be allowed to develop and die away before the grass is cut in July. As with all bulbs it is essential to allow the leaves to die away completely and naturally.

One of the earliest to appear is *C. autumnale* with pale mauve to purple flowers which tend to splay on maturity. This species has doubled forms in white and pink which are superior to the single. The species *C. speciosum* and its hybrids are also early flowering and offer the widest range of colour and some of the finest flowers of all. The flowers of the type are large and globular up to 12in in height, the colour is variable ranging from pale lilac pink with a white throat to intense carmine. Some of the hybrids, mainly crosses with the tessellated species are spectacular plants giving bright splashes of colour from their large open cups.

133

One of the finest named varieties is the Giant which gives a profusion of delicate pink flowers. This is a vigorous and strong grower, ideal for naturalising in grass. For deeper colour *C. atrorubens* with its crimson purple petals is one of the best while *C. speciosum album* is the cleanest of the whites.

Late Summer Flowering

Some late flowering plants are generally accepted as being chancy on the probability of flowering as profusely as one would wish. The late flowering *Liriope muscari* is a case in point. While most books and catalogues will give its requirements as a sandy soil and sunny situation, the necessity of frequent division to ensure a good show of flowers is rarely mentioned. Like many of the clump-forming herbaceous subjects which give poor flowers from congested plants, the liriope will go one better and fail to flower at all.

This little evergreen from Japan is an absolute treasure for the front of the border. Making arching tufts of shining green leaves which are decorative throughout the year, it is an invaluable plant where permanent plantings are required. In late summer beaded spikes of violet flowers are pushed up on extremely strong stems. These closely packed flowers are long lasting and will continue well into October. The species *L. graminifolia* is similar but more vigorous and can on occasion become invasive. One of the most delightful of all is a miniature form with white flowers encrusting an extremely strong stem that is almost black in colour. This is a first-class plant to set among alpines and seems to do well in sun or shade.

Two other blue flowered plants that can be relied on for late summer is the grey leaved *Perovskia atriplicifolia* and the aromatic *Caryopteris clandonensis*. The former is a shrubby plant of the sage family, with beautiful grey-green leaves set on white stems. In late summer the plant is set with spires of lavender blue tubular flowers that last for many weeks. A variety Blue Mist has almost pure blue flowers rather earlier than the type. These are splendid plants for chalky soil and maritime districts where they can be exposed to full sun. So many of the late summer flowering plants are aromatic and the caryopteris has pleasant pungent leaves. Although a first-class plant it is seldom seen, perhaps because it is only reliably hardy in favoured districts or warm corners. When sited favourably this bushy plant will spread widely, its long lax stems reaching out to make a clump some 4ft wide. The small flowers create a smother of bloom and are an extraordinary attractive shade of blue. This is an ideal plant for associating with the pink *Nerine bowdenii*.

Some of the physostegias make a rather leisurely start but when in full flower they are well worth waiting for. More often, they are known as the Obedient Plant because the tiers of pink flowers are attached to the stalks by a sort of ball and socket arrangement and stay where put when moved to an angle. All varieties have running roots and make a fairly solid clump with intense colour in various shades of pink. There are white cultivars but these are not such good plants. *P. virginiana* vivid is one of the smallest and probably one of the most useful in the small gardens. The form known as Summer Spire is much taller and more easily damaged by summer storms but this is another plant that has good winter stems. These turn deep crimson as the season progresses.

A welcome aristocrat from Japan that also flowers in late summer is *Kirengeshoma palmata*. One always expects the waxy yellow flowers to open more fully but anticipation coupled with their reticence only makes them all the more desirable. Everything about this shade-loving plant is distinguished, from the slender purple stems and the vine-like leaves of the nodding sulphur coloured bells. This is a plant that needs careful placing and would look out of place anywhere except in the shade of trees or a wall. It must never be allowed to dry out at the roots. Best grown against a sunny wall the Cape Figwort, *Phygelius capensis,* will reach 6ft or so and flower persistently until October. The individual tubular blooms of coral red are quite small, but seen in mass or hanging on sprays they are most effective.

Most polygonums are noted for their deep delving roots but the late flowering *P. campanulatum* has roots that only penetrate an inch or so. Initially this plant makes a thick mat of crinkled leaves that is completely weed proof. In the late summer a mass of candy pink flowers is supported by shining red stems while the basal leaves continue to provide good cover. Being a more robust plant with shallow roots it does require occasional watering in dry spells.

6

Winter

Winter with all its attendant nastiness of frost and snow can provide much interest in the garden in the way of flowers and foliage. Even at the turn of the year the well-furnished garden should be able to provide some colour and interest from aconites, hellebores and winter jasmine.

Snowdrops

Snowdrops will always be thought of as giving the first real show of the year and for the enthusiast and collector the first blooms appear as early as October, but it is *Galanthus nivalis* the tiny commoner of February that is best appreciated in our gardens. Being the one species that is cheap and plentiful enough to plant in mass, it is ideal for making wide drifts and thrives on clay or chalk. The whole nivalis family is as reliable as it is charming and includes some fine vigorous cultivars that are worth looking out for and planting in small groups where they can be left to increase and be enjoyed in the winter months. Most of them are taller and more showy than the type and will do as well in an open situation as in light shade.

One of the strangest is *G. atkinsii,* a tall snowdrop with globular flowers that will usually be in bloom by mid-January. Its flowers will usually be identified by one malformed petal although this does not detract from the general beauty of the plant.

The seedling *G. n. S.* Arnott has flowers that are perfectly formed and is also a vigorous and reliable plant. Originating in an Irish garden, the Straffan snowdrop is a late bloomer that increases freely once planted in a soil to its liking. Moving or dividing clumps is a relatively easy matter. This is best done immediately after flowering which means that one does not have to probe about searching for hidden bulbs. They are all such good tempered plants that no harm comes to them if they are dug up and moved when in full flower, providing their roots are not allowed to dry out.

There is a surprising diversity of form, even among this one group of snowdrops. Many of them have double forms, intricately patterned with green while *G. n. viridapicis* is identified by the distinctive green spot at the tip of each outer petal. One that sometimes needs a little extra care is *G. n. scharlokii.* This is furnished with long spathes that stand up like donkey's ears and is generally regarded as more strange than beautiful.

Buttercup Family

No gardener can afford to ignore any family of plants that has flowers of one kind or another for at least ten months of the year;

and the buttercup tribe can contribute with some very early flowers.

It is difficult to know when the season starts with this family. Early in the year the various forms of hellebore are in flower and continue to display their strange colours until May. The gold laquered eranthis are the first flowers to appear above ground in late winter closely followed by the various forms of *Ranunculus ficara*. This tiny plant is a most valuable addition to the winter garden, although its reputation as a coloniser does not endear it to the tidy gardener. After blooming for weeks at a time of the year when there is little else about, it will obligingly disappear underground until the following winter. To gardeners of more informal persuasion the mottled heart-shaped leaves are a definite asset and are at home nestling between clumps of small bulbs and early spring foliage. The more common yellow form is certainly the most weedy but a fine white variety with a yellow centre and a blue sheen to the undersides of the petals is more restrained. The two double forms usually do not spread at all and are best increased by dividing the tiny tubers after flowering. Both doubles are good enough for a place in any rock garden, one having a pronounced green centre to its closely packed petals.

Hellebores

The hellebores, that other popular family of winter flowering plants, need heavy feeding and should be top dressed after flowering with bonemeal and bulky organic manures, or compost.

Most books and catalogues will describe the hellebores as shade-loving plants but they will do remarkably well in most open situations. Thorough preparation of the soil in depth, good drainage and ample feeding are the main requirements for the strong annual growth that one expects from these plants.

The largest and most statuesque of these is *H. corsicus* whose large trusses of pale green bells last for many weeks; when they finally fade, they are replaced by some of the most decorative seed capsules that any plant can provide. This outstanding plant has the lightest coloured leaves of all the hellebores and they are decorative the whole year round.

After the seed has ripened the central flowering stems die away and are replaced by a mass of new light green leaves from the central crown. This cycle of growth is also to be found in *H. foetidus*, smaller in flower but even finer in form being of upright habit with tapering deeply cut leaves that are almost black in colour. When in flower there is something to be said for planting these in drifts but both are worthy of planting as single specimens to show off their fine outlines.

The non-shrubby hellebores, those which annually send up flowers and leaves from the base, includes the well known Christmas rose and the easier and more floriferous lenten roses. For good ground cover the large fingered leaves are excellent throughout the summer but become so tattered and unsightly in winter that they are best removed just before the new flowering buds push through the soil. Nurserymen will usually supply lenten roses in a wide but unspecified range of colours and all of these are good ranging through creams, greens, rosy pinks to deep plum. Those with spots at the base of the petals are especially beautiful as are the plum coloured forms which have exquisite golden stamens. For the collector of hellebores there are many fine and sometimes rare species to be had. Most of these are no more demanding than the commoner kinds, providing they are given conditions that all the family like. The rare purples, *H. atrorubens* and *H. torquatus* and the primrose coloured *H. kochii* are well worth searching for, and for those who prefer something rather special in green flowering *H. cyclophyllus* and *H. viridis* will give much pleasure.

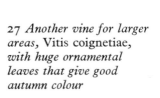
Page 141   26 *The purple
leaved vine,* Vitis vinifera
purpurea, *is one of the
best climbers for foliage
effect*

27 *Another vine for larger
areas,* Vitis coignetiae,
*with huge ornamental
leaves that give good
autumn colour*

Page 142   28 *The Himalayan thistle,*
Morina longifolia, *is an elegant
plant with white flowers set in thorny
bracts which later turn to pink*
29   (left) *Rising from a basal
rosette of white leaves, the enormous
flowering stems of* Verbascum
bombyciferum *are studded with
lemon yellow flowers*

Euphorbias

Anyone who has grown euphorbias will know that at the turn of the year *E. wulfenii* is already arching the tips of its flowering shoots in readiness for its huge green croziers of spring. By this curious practice it is possible to tell roughly what kind of flowering season lies ahead although not all the soft shoots survive a hard winter spell. This spurge is a plant that is either loved or hated but whatever one's feelings, its boldness with or without flowers makes it one of the most useful architectural plants in the garden. One specimen will be enough in a small garden as fully grown it will be at least 3ft across with its lower branches sweeping the ground.

The biennial spurge *E. lathyrus* is a prodigious seeder but the seedlings are of such good colour and bold form that they are worth keeping for winter decoration and rooting out unwanted plants in the spring.

Unflowered plants after a season's growth will vary in height from between 1ft to 3ft and have slender glaucous stems clothed with linear leaves with a prominent white stripe. This is a striking foliage plant for winter where height is needed and will quickly recover from severe frost which attacks, but does not destroy or mar, its fine leaves.

For bold winter foliage of a different order *E. robbiae* is capable of carpeting the ground between shrubs with neat rosettes of shining deep green leaves within a short time. This one is a wanderer and will colonise and thrive in the most inhospitable conditions even pottering along the base of a boundary hedge where there is little light or nourishment. Surprisingly, these three spring flowering spurges will thrive on a poor soil as well as any. If the soil is inclined to be heavy so much the better, for

I

E. wulfenii and *E. lathyrus* are stout plants and like roses they need firm soil round the roots to prevent them being rocked by the wind.

Winter Foliage

Decorative foliage plays an important part in furnishing the winter garden and some of the finest leaves are provided by the variegated arum. This plant does not appear above ground until late autumn and obligingly dies down and rests during the summer months when there is no lack of other subjects to catch the eye.

Arum pictum is a form of our native cuckoo pint, or lords and ladies, and has the same arrow shaped leaves, except that they are marbled with grey and white and will survive any weather. They will recover their good looks quickly from the most searing frosts or weighty snow falls.

Although the main reason for growing this plant is its foliage, the typical arum flowers that appear in summer are followed by spikes of orange berries which are rather showy and worth having. Providing enough moisture is available and slugs are kept at bay the clumps should remain in beauty until the following spring, the best leaves being from plants in sunny positions. Two variations are commonly available *Arum italicum pictum* and *A. marmoratum*. The former is without doubt the better garden plant having more striking variegation, and better flowers if these are also to be considered.

In winter evergreen foliage plants begin to give full value as permanent furnishing to the border. Some of the most successful of these from the colour standpoint are the blue-leaved plants which retain their colour remarkably well. Unlike the grey-leaved plants whose leaves are clothed with minute hairs and consequently look the worse for wear in damp weather the blues retain their good looks whatever the conditions.

The most striking effect of all with leaves of this colour can be had with the best forms of *Ruta graveloens*, Jackman's Blue. This small shrub should be grown much more widely for its strong colour and compact habit. In all but the worst winters it will retain its fresh leaves through until early spring when the searing winds will begin to scorch the edges. At the end of March when new growth is beginning the plant can be cut hard back to the base of the previous year's growth. The immediate effect of such brutal treatment is hideous but the stump will quickly put on a mass of fresh young growth which will develop into a rounded dome of blue. This hard annual pruning always results in compact shapely bushes, without it the plants become straggly and show unsightly masses of leggy stems.

Almost as good in colour but displaying fine foliage the whole year round, *Hebe pinguifolia pagei* make a wide prostrate mat of blue-grey leaves. This is a good ground cover plant and the thick smooth textured leaf will tolerate any conditions in town or country. A light clipping after flowering is all the attention that this plant requires to keep it compact and neat.

There are two grasses with steely blue leaves that are reasonably good for much of the winter and neither of these are likely to spread or get out of hand. The smaller of the two, *Festuca ovina glauca*, a sheep's fescue, make dense tufts 6in or so high and is an extremely useful edging plant. This grass has some of the neatest of all flower heads and is splendid material for tightening up and giving form to loose plantings of annuals. The larger grass *Helictotrichon sempervirens* is a first-rate spot plant with narrow arching leaves some 18in high with 3ft flower stems. It may need an occasional tidying up in the winter months if it is to look its best. This simply consists of removing the dead leaves which come away easily from the crown.

The delicate ferny foliage of the aceanas is much tougher than it looks and its wiry stems will creep over earth or stone. There are numerous forms of this sun-loving plant with coloured leaves ranging from bronze to metallic glaucous green. Its durable qualities make it an ideal plant for the edge of a stone or gravel path since it will not resent being occasionally trodden on. The flowers are small and inconspicuous, often sporting burr-like spines. It will thrive in the poorest soils.

Some have unusual blue-green foliage, but that of the best and largest of them, *A. glaucophylla,* dies away in mid winter. At its best this is a magnificent trailing plant with swirls of finely cut blue foliage supporting crimson stems and burrs. There are smaller ground-hugging forms such as *A. buchananii,* but though evergreen these are not of such good colour.

7

Trees and Shrubs

With so many improved forms of garden plants today, there is little excuse for planting poor specimens and none at all when it comes to permanent things like trees or shrubs. Nurserymen in their catalogue descriptions are sometimes apt to be a little optimistic about size, colour and hardiness of plants. Good nurserymen produce good plants of the best strains, and it is this type of plant that should be sought out. Lilacs for instance can easily be rather washy and undistinguished, poor things beside good varieties with blooms of clear intense colour. While so many hybrid flowers have a reputation for lacking the fragrance of their parents, the scent of lilacs is as fresh as ever.

A lesser consideration, but one worth remembering when planning the placing and choice of trees is the general decorative effect in the dormant season and the interest that a well marked bark can give. Most deciduous trees are bare for at least five months of the year; and, particularly in a small garden, the importance of making everything possible earn its keep in the off season cannot be stressed too highly. The position of such a tree is important. Planted fairly near the house or at least near a path one travels daily, it may be enjoyed to the full and will give much pleasure, especially if one of the more colourful barks are chosen.

Maples

Again proper siting in relation to the position of the winter sun plays a great part in getting full value and lasting enjoyment from them. The paperbark maple *Acer griseum* needs backlighting for full effect of the glowing colour of its peeling skin. Snakebark varieties on the other hand are best sited with the sun full on them. Their striated barks will glisten on a bright winter day. The snakebark which originated in China and America will grow reasonably well in chalky soils. These are ideal trees for the small modern garden, since they are of medium size and shapely habit.

Acer pennsylvanicum, known locally in the States as moosewood, has conspicuous white striated trunk and branches and rich coral coloured twigs.

The species from China are most valuable additions to the garden, the most attractive being *A. laxiflorum* with purple red trunk and white striations and twigs that are pillar-box red when young. *A. Davidii* is another fine specimen with a tendency to spread outwards. It has dark green leaves which colour to yellow, red and purple. The third Chinaman is *A. Grosseri* with good markings and autumn colour; its variety *hersii* has the added charm of conspicuous fruits in pendulous racemes up to 5in long with almost horizontal keys.

There are two maples from Japan with good bark. *Acer capillipes* is a small tree with striated bark and young growths of coral red while *A. rufinerve* has green trunk and branches with distinctive diamond-shaped markings in greyish brown. Both of

148

these colour well in the autumn but are perhaps best on a lime-free soil as are most plants that originate from Japan.

One last maple which differs from all others is the paper bark, *A. griseum.* The trunk and primary branches of this tree peel back to reveal bright orange bark beneath and is most unusual and effective. This maple is the exception when placing it in relation to the sun, for the finest effect will be had when the sun is behind the tree, shining through the curling bark.

Coloured Stems

In search of colour for the winter garden, a striking effect can be had from the coloured stems of some of the hardy shrubs. The young stems of some of the willows give some of the best results and are easy to grow providing they are given a soil that does not dry out. The pendulous golden yellow stems of the weeping willow *Salix* are one of the most beautiful of all sights in the winter garden. For those who cannot accommodate such a large and vigorous tree, *Salix alba vitellina* is a good choice. The young shoots of this small tree are a rich egg yellow and make magnificent contrast to a dark coniferous background. Pollarding every second year of the shrubby species will ensure a plentiful supply of fresh young shoots. This practice is most effective where the stems can be cut down to the stool, but can be used to advantage with some of the smaller trees such as *Salix daphnoides* or *S. acutifolia.* Both these willows have unusual purple-violet shoots covered with a white bloom, the latter differing by its darker damson tints. The vigorous shrubby willow, *S. irrorata* puts on a mass of long green shoots in summer which gradually turn purple and make a striking winter show when powdered with their white bloom.

Orange and scarlet stems are an asset in any winter planting and a form of the white willow *S. alba chermesina* can give brilliant orange-scarlet stems particularly if hard pruned annually or every second year.

Of all the coloured stems available those of the shrubby dog-woods are the brightest of all and outshine any other bark commonly grown. In winter they take on intense tones and being suitable for most soils they can play an important part in the winter garden.

The red barked dogwoods, *Cornus alba* and its varieties, are the best known of all for their brilliant red stems and give some of the most striking winter colour. These shrubs eventually form dense thickets and are ideal for covering large areas. The variety *Cornus alba sibirica* has the most striking brilliant crimson branches, but its variegated form, with broad white edges to its leaves, is a better garden plant where food foliage is required. For golden variegation *C. alba spaethii* is the best form.

Some of the brambles have startling white stems and are at their best in the winter months. They do however put on tremendous growth and their lax stems need a great deal of space. Alternatively they can be trained up poles and then allowed to cascade to the ground. Having branching stems which reach 8ft or so, *Rubus cockburnianus* has some of the best stems of all. These are pure white and on first sight appear to have received a coat of whitewash. *Rubus biflorus* is a similar plant, but *R. thibetanus* is rather smaller and has 6ft stems clothed with a bluish-white deposit. This bramble has fine large leaves, dark green above and white felted on the undersides. As with all brambles, old wood and spent stems should be cut out from the base to keep these shrubs fresh and shapely.

Bright green stems can be introduced by planting the quick growing *Leycesteria formosa,* another shrub that gives a superb summer show of leaves, flower and fruit. The hollow bamboo-like stems of this plant are surprisingly hardy and last well into the winter before the tips become browned by frost.

Certain species of roses especially *R. sericea pteracantha* are endowed with magnificent translucent spines that are almost as colourful as the flowers they bear. For best effect these should be planted so that they can be viewed with the low winter sun shining through the broad blood-red thorns on the young shoots.

Freaks

Freaks of nature are rarely sought after as permanent subjects for the garden, although certain of them, like fasciated flowers and stems, are harmless enough and their interesting shape makes them conversation pieces. Several trees and shrubs with strange and fascinating forms have become firm, if uncommon, favourites and since their strangeness lies in the formation of the branches and twigs they make ideal backgrounds to the winter garden.

Salix matsudana tortuosa, is a willow of great winter beauty, whose sinuous branches curl and twist skyward and are superb against a winter sky. The upright habit of this tree makes it suitable for any reasonably sized garden and like all willows its rate of growth is fairly rapid.

A better shrub for the smaller garden with similar habit is the corkscrew hazel, *Corylus avellana contorta.* The branches and twigs of this shrub are even more sinuous and since it is an altogether more lowly and spreading shrub, it is an obvious choice when something of winter interest is needed near the house. In summer it can be a mediocre plant but as soon as its twisted framework is fully exposed it is transformed into one of the most beautiful and interesting outlines in the winter garden.

The beech family also has one member, in *Fagus tortuosa,* with the same twisting branches but with pendulous tips. This is seen much less often, but is a good tree for a large garden.

Winter Flowering Shrubs

Shrubs that begin their flowering season when most leaves have just fallen are few and far between. Several of the viburnums begin to show their white flowers in early December and some like *V. tinus* and *V. bodnantense* contribute a hint of pink.

The fleeting yellow blooms of the winter jasmine appear as early as any but are inclined to look shabby during severe frost.

By far the most imposing of all the winter flowering shrubs is Mahonia Charity, a tall arching evergreen of striking appearance. This hybrid between *M. japonica* and *M. lomariifolia* retains its gaunt and erect habit from the latter parent but is topped by such good leaves and handsome flower spikes that it is worth using as a background shrub and masking the stems by some low growing evergreen.

For dealing with large areas under trees the common *M. aquifolium* grows to a convenient height and obligingly spreads by suckers, eventually making complete ground cover. This is also a useful and inexpensive shrub for game coverts and looks attractive the whole year through. In early spring the bushes are liberally laden with fluffy yellow flowers and these are followed by the bronze coloured new growths. Being a species of considerable variation *M. aquifolium* has given rise to some good forms, the best being *M. a. undulata*. This is a rather upright form and will eventually reach 6ft, remaining thick enough at the base to make fine evergreen hedges; in winter the shining leaves will take on bronze and crimson tints.

The most fragrant of all is *M. japonica*, a superb shrub that for many years was often confused and wrongly listed in some catalogues with *M. bealei* to which it is related. With a lily of the valley fragrance and a preference for some shade this form has the longest flower spikes of all. It is in flower from December to April and like all mahonias is followed by a show of black berries coated with a plum-like bloom.

Although the cultivated forms do not sucker so freely as *M. aquifolium* there will usually be one or two pieces at the base of each plant that can be pulled away and used as propagation material.

Viburnums

There is scarcely a month in the year when one or other of the great family of viburnums does not have something to offer in the way of flowers or berries. Even in the dark months of December and January the evergreen varieties can be relied on to brighten the scene with handsome foliage while the popular Laurustinus, *V. tinus*, bears masses of pink and white flowers from November to early spring. So-called improved forms of this variety are not always completely hardy and for general garden work the type is difficult to better.

All the winter flowering forms bloom for a long period and one of the best of these is *V. bodnantense*, a vigorous hybrid with pink tinted flowers that have a delicious fragrance and are seldom damaged by frost. The parents of this hybrid are fine winter flowering plants in their own right, *V. fragrans* and *V. grandiflorum*. The former produces a succession of small scented pale pink blossoms from late autumn until early spring, while *V. grandiflorum* sports much larger flowers of a deeper shade of pink opening from attractive crimson buds.

From April onwards through to early summer there are so many viburnums available that making a choice of one from so many good plants can be difficult. Fortunately there are half a dozen or so outstanding garden forms that are so good that a space for one or more should be found in every garden. Most are easily grown and tolerant of any soil eventually making big

shrubs excellent for back of the border. Our native guelder rose
V. opulus and its forms are all beautiful in flower and fruit particularly the cultivar *V. opulus sterile,* the snowball tree, which is a
plant of outstanding merit. Often grown and only of medium
size *V. carlesii* has typical showy pink buds which open to pure
white sweetly scented globular clusters.

The tomentosum group are shrubs of great character with wide
spreading horizontal branches that carry masses of bloom in
layers on the upper surfaces. In early summer at the height of the
flowering period these are a magnificent sight giving the effect
of snow laden branches. The cultivars Lanarth and *mariesii* are
both fine forms free flowering and with a bonus of crimson leaves
in the autumn.

For a genus that is primarily grown for its flowers and fragrance, several kinds put on a striking display of berries. Outstanding among these is a tall growing form *V. betulifolium* with
large bunches of berries like redcurrants. These are borne in
such profusion that the long branches are often arched over with
the weight of the fruits which persist well into the winter.

The evergreen dwarf *V. davidii* has bright turquoise blue
berries and leathery dark green leaves. Together with *V. judii*
these are probably the two best for the small garden and will
give a long period of fruit and flower. Red berries that eventually
turn black are produced on *V. rhytidophyllum* but it is the long
deeply veined leaves which are so attractive in this plant. While
it will grow happily in heavy soils it does not like wind and is
probably best planted against a wall. The wrinkled leaves which
are evergreen are decorative enough to embellish any wall and
have buff felted undersides. It should be remembered when
planting viburnums for berries that best results are obtained by
planting two or more together for cross pollination, certain kinds
like *V. davidii* will be most disappointing if this is not borne in
mind.

Early Spring Flowering Shrubs

In early spring before the rush of young green leaves when borders are still dark and sombre the sight of an early bloom however simple is regarded with far more pleasure than the most colourful of flowers at the height of the growing season. Shrubs with this propensity can make a fine splash of colour in an otherwise dull scene and there are several of medium size that can be grown in most gardens.

One group of shrubs that fit well into such positions is the corylopsis, relatives of the witch-hazels. These hardy shrubs represented commonly by about six varieties are ideal for smaller moderate size gardens since the tallest rarely exceeds 15ft in height and when the flowers are over gives a good background of hazel-like leaves. The primrose-colour flowers are borne in drooping racemes and hang from March to April and if a position can be found for them where the sun will catch the flowers while leaving the background in shade the result is most striking. Unfortunately late spring frosts are inclined to cause some damage to the blooms but given the shelter of neighbouring shrubs this need not be too severe.

Another shrub useful for this purpose, represented by two varieties, is *Stachyurus chinensis* and *S. praecox.* Of the two the former is the more vigorous and will make a tree of 10ft in height and 8ft across. The catkin-like flowers hang in stiff ropes from February to April. *Stachyurus praecox* is the one most commonly seen in gardens and comes into flower a fortnight or so earlier. With its rather stiff habit and eye-catching qualities of cream flowers on red shoots it makes a good spot plant for the early border.

Shrubs that flower between November and March are the very bones of the winter garden and many of these have a fragrance that announces their presence and carries for yards on a still winter day. Some scents of winter are so subtle that one is aware only of the slightest whiff, while others like the wintersweet are so strong that awareness of the fragrance comes before sight of the flower. This shrub which was generally known as *Chimonanthus fragrans* should now be called *C. praecox* and is most valuable especially when planted near the house. Although classed as a shrub of spreading habit it is easy enough to train against a wall and if given full sun on a west wall it will return this kindness by producing a mass of fragrant waxy bells for much of the winter.

A well grown witch-hazel in full bloom must be the most brilliant of all the winter shrubs. The one that is usually grown is *Hamamelis mollis* and is good enough to grace the finest garden. A variety of this species *H. m. pallida* has much larger and brighter lemon yellow flowers that are densely packed along the branches. The scents of the witch-hazels are distinctive and spicy although they do not carry so well as those of the wintersweet. Another yellow flowering shrub blooming at the same time and which should be in every garden is the mahonia, doubly valuable because of its splendid evergreen leaves. Some varieties like the selected forms of *M. japonica* are especially good for flower and fragrance but tend to make rather wide bushes. These are best kept in bounds by cutting out the flower heads when the season is over. This should also increase the amount of bloom the following year. One of the best mahonias for the small garden is *M. aquifolium undulata* which has smaller sprays of leaves, is of compact habit and bears fluffy heads of pale yellow flowers with a lily of the valley scent.

A dwarf shrub with evergreen leaves that is every bit as good as the mahonias is the sarcocca. This shrub is always neat and fresh with tiny inconspicuous flowers that give off a fragrance reminiscent of vanilla. Since these low growing shrubs will thrive in the deepest shade, they make first-class ground cover under trees or between larger shrubs and are good on lime. Like the flowers of the sarcoccas many of the more fragrant winter blooms are small and insignificant. Two bush honeysuckles fall into this category and if not showy enough for an important position are good background material.

Lonicera fragrantissima and *L. standishii* are dense shrubs with small cream flowers, the former being semi-evergreen and the latter bearing red berries in June. These two are the parents of a more vigorous hybrid *L. purpusii* which is now generally regarded as a more superior plant for the garden.

Towards the end of February, the first blooms of the mezeron appear, thickly clustered on naked stems to add colour to the winter garden. The colours of the common *Daphne mezerum* combine well with other things flowering at this time and add a touch of brilliance that few of the others have. Being a native of the woodlands of Europe, it appreciates the close company of other plants and always seems to be at home in the cottage garden. Mezeron bark is said to have had its place in folk medicine and it was probably grown for these utilitarian virtues rather than its brilliant winter display.

In the larger and more formal garden, they are not always easy to please and although one may try to reproduce woodland conditions for their benefit, some of the best plants are to be seen growing in cold, limey clays enriched with a little manure. Some protection from full sun is advisable especially on the soft bark of the stems which may split if baked by a full glare. Damage to any part of the stems should be avoided at all costs and while flowering shoots cut for the house last well in water this should not be encouraged. Cutting or pruning usually results in the plant dying back and in some cases this can be fatal.

Given the right conditions a healthy plant will make an erect bush some 2–3ft in height and bloom from early February to late March. The flowers, which thickly encrust the previous year's young wood, have tiny recurving petals and distinctive stamens.

The fragrance is strong and particularly noticeable on a winter's day when it has little competition in the garden. As with most winter flowering plants, the best show is put on during mild spells but frost rarely harms the blooms and if planted in the right situation the damage from drying winds should be negligible.

This daphne has a deeper pink form and a white which bears yellow berries, unlike the pink which has shining red fruits. A supposedly improved form, *D. grandiflora,* has larger deep pink flowers and the peculiarity of flowering in September. The berries, though attractive, are poisonous; but it is a lucky gardener who can save them from the birds as the finches will eat them when green.

If stock is to be increased it is worth giving some protection to allow the berries to ripen, which they normally do in July. If seed is gathered and freshly sown the rate of germination is fairly good and from these the best plants are obtained. None of the daphnes are long lived and the life-span of the grafted forms is said to be even shorter. They are also notoriously bad movers and a young seedling transplanted direct from the pot complete with soil ball round the roots stands a much better chance of survival. The rate of growth is slow which makes them ideal shrubs for the small garden but in the right conditions, they are not so slow as some authorities would suggest and in a few years make a comfortable sized bush that never fails to brighten the winter scene.

Catkins

Catkins of one kind or another are with us for much of the year but it is only when the leaves have fallen that their full qualities are appreciated. Indeed some of the summer flowering catkins tend to be missed altogether including the long green tassels of

Page 159   30 *The lenten roses,* H. orientalis, *have a wide range of colour and are in flower over a long period*

31 *Our native* H. foetidus *is a statuesque plant in flower from January until May*
32 (*left*) Helleborus lividus, *slightly tender but worth trying in a sheltered spot*

Page 160   33 *The silver-leaved pear,* Pyrus salicifolia pendula, *is an ideal tree for the small garden; with its slow growth and elegant habit it rarely outgrows its allotted space. The specimen in the picture is clipped annually with shears*

the evergreen *Itea ilicifolia*. This is a Chinese holly-like shrub small enough for most gardens but preferring some shade and protection from adjacent trees or the shelter of a wall. If the latter position is chosen plenty of humus should be added to the soil before planting. Dryness at the roots is a condition it will not tolerate if it is to look completely happy.

The long silky tassels of the much larger evergreen *Garrya elliptica* are at their best in January and February and with this shrub the catkins are shown to advantage against the dark oval leaves. The best catkins appear on the male bushes and will grow to 6in or more in mild districts. Catkins on the female bushes rarely exceed 4in but both sexes should be planted if it is required to fruit. Given the shelter of a wall and some winter protection in its first years it develops into a substantial dark green shrub that will help to give solidity to an otherwise leafless garden. A south or west wall is usually recommended and such a position will give the best flowers; sunless walls are by no means hopeless provided they are not too exposed to bitter winds.

Besides being rather tender in their first years garryas do not take kindly to root disturbance, and container grown plants should always be used and planted in spring. Unfortunately it cannot be recommended with unreserved enthusiasm, for in spite of its handsome appearance and ease of cultivation once established, its growth can be too rapid for many situations. Fully grown it will reach 15ft in height with a 12ft spread. A large area of wall is needed for these dimensions and if positioned too near a window it will need constant cutting back and consequently lose its shape. Any pruning and trimming should be done before new growth starts.

This may be necessary to remove some of the leaves that have been disfigured by frost and remain unsightly if left on for the following season.

꧁꧂

Trees for the Small Garden

At the beginning of each planting season, one of the most frequent subjects on which advice is sought is that of suitable trees for small gardens. Too often the question is put by the impatient who want a mature tree within a few years, usually to be grown in the smallest possible space. No matter what advice is given, they will plant a fast growing weeping willow which will outgrow its allotted space within a few years.

Beautiful as it is this is one of a number of trees that should never be introduced into the small garden or planted near buildings. Nothing will thrive under the branches of a mature willow and the wandering roots will rob the soil of moisture and nutrients for yards around. Away from water a weeping willow rarely looks happy and is prone to more nasty pests and unsightly diseases than any other commonly grown tree, a full list of which merits attention from the would-be willow planter.

If one must have a weeping tree in a small garden something more restrained like the silver leaved pear, *Pyrus salicifolia pendula*, has all the qualities necessary for a trouble free and highly decorative specimen tree. Its one drawback is its painfully slow rate of growth in its early years but once the roots have settled in it will put on satisfactory growth.

The willow-shaped leaves of this pear are clothed with silvery down in early spring and the beautiful but insignificant flowers bloom at the end of March or early April. The calyx and stalks of each flower is also covered with white hairs which tends to blend the flowers in with the leaves. Small fruits appear after the flowers but these are gritty and tasteless and fall to the ground before ripening.

A good specimen usually arrives from the nursery as a feathered sapling with widely spaced branches along the whole length of the trunk. While such a specimen may at first appear to be rather thin and whippy it will allow for training and eventually make a better tree than if grown from a top-heavy standard. Trained as an umbrella and contrasted against a darker hedge or shrubs, it is a splendid thing.

Another small tree suitable for most gardens is *Arbutus unedo.* With the exception of the strawberry tree which rarely grows much above 15ft, the remainder of the hardy members of the arbutus family are rather too large for the average garden, but where space permits they are one of the most warming sights in the winter garden and seen at their best in a low evening sun. The impact of a warm light on the sinuous trunks, feathered with peeling bark in shades of cinnamon, terracotta and lime green rivals the brightest of autumn colours.

This family of ericaceous trees and shrubs all with glossy dark evergreen leaves are remarkable for their ability to thrive on limey soils and their toleration of our winters although they are mostly natives of the eastern mediterranean countries. In the soft climate of south-west Ireland *A. unedo,* the strawberry tree, is like the fuchsia naturalised. This species has flowers remarkably like those of the lily of the valley and blooms from October to December. The insipid strawberry-like fruits take a whole year to ripen and are still hanging on the tree when the succeeding year's flowers open. With its bushy growth and warm brown trunk this is the best species to plant in the small garden.

For best effects of peeling bark *A. andrachne* and its hybrid *A. andrachnoides,* a cross between the former and *A. unedo,* are superb. Both have the typical cinnamon red trunks and branches with an underlay of lime green and while they can be rather difficult to establish and a little tender when young they are perfectly hardy as older specimens. A mature planting of several species is one of the finest sights a garden can offer on a fine winter afternoon.

One other shrub with branches that can give much the same effect is *Stuartia sinensis*, a plant for lime-free soils. This flowers in July and August giving a long succession of blooms and in the right soil will give rich autumn colour.

Thorns

Thorns are not particularly showy plants unless in flower or fruit but the wonderful show that they can put on in a good autumn justifies their use on cold windswept sites where more demanding subjects might fail. This large family of small trees and shrubs has some seventy species and forms available for garden use that are of medium size and extremely hardy. Besides giving a brilliant show of berries at the end of the season many forms have good autumn leaf colour.

While the shining red haws will always be a favourite part of the winter scene it is not often realised that there are also species with blue, black, yellow and orange fruits. Few trees are more colourful in autumn than the small but heavy headed *Crataegus prunifolia* with its scarlet tinted leaves and plump berries, both of which fall in late October.

Gluttonous blackbirds are the curse of the forms with the more luscious berries, they will begin systematically to strip a tree the moment the haws are ripe. The berries of *C. monogyna* of which there are a number of forms are at least left alone until severe weather sets in. This form is still one of the best boundary hedging plants, thorny and impenetrable without being untidy.

Although the crataegus family are commonly known as thorns and some like cockspur thorn have spines up to 3in long there are thornless varieties which are much safer as specimen plants for lawns or situations near paths. For use as specimen plants there are among the species *C. monogyna* and *C. oxycantha* single and double forms with pink or crimson flowers, although these can look rather heavy if not given the right setting.

Considering they are such easy and adaptable plants, propagation is a rather long-winded affair. Cuttings are notoriously difficult to strike and the accepted method is by seed. This usually takes two years to germinate and should be stratified for eighteen months. Possibly this could be speeded up by refrigeration but it is not a process recommended to the ordinary gardener.

It cannot be said that any of the thorns have particularly attractive bark but the knarled appearance of the trunk of many varieties as they begin to mature is an attraction that could be utilised in many gardens.

Weeping Forms

For variety of shape and habit some of the most beautiful trees and shrubs that we can grow in our gardens successfully are those of weeping or pendulous habit. The weeping willow is probably the most beautiful of all at any season and the one most commonly grown, but as we have seen it is one that needs water and a large garden if it is to develop naturally over the years.

For a small tree with accent on the downward sweep of branches the weeping form of the white mulberry has branches which cascade to ground level and makes a splendid specimen tree, interesting in shape especially when leafless. Blossom is all important on some trees and for those who like their quota of showy flowers, weeping forms of many of the popular flowering trees are available. *Laburnum pendulum* is a most graceful tree and small enough to fit into most gardens.

There are several weeping cherries including *Prunus subhirtella pendula rubra* with thin drooping branches and deep rose flowers.

These are a lovely sight at the height of the flowering period with cascades of white and pink falling to the ground.

Evergreens of weeping habit are good for a focal point in the small garden and usually strong enough in shape to draw the eye but not too tall to be disproportionate with the surroundings. The hollies rank among the best of these and the weeping form of the common green holly is quite magnificent especially the female form when loaded with berries. Another which berries freely is Perry's Silver Weeping Holly with brilliant variegation to the leaves.

A neat evergreen for the small lawn is the pendulous variety of the western hemlock, *Tsuga canadensis pendula*. Its slow growth and interesting branch formation has much to recommend it.

The rare weeping form of the Blue Cedar is a most striking tree and best planted where it will have ample space for its angled branches to sweep the ground. Equally striking and of unusual shape is the weeping Wellingtonia, *Sequoiadendron pendula*, a giant among trees and only for the largest gardens. Many of the weeping forms of our more common trees, beech, ash and elm take up rather too much space for the average garden of today but can make ideal specimens for a large lawn or wild garden where they can be seen to advantage and their roots and sweeping branches will not interfere with the surrounding plantings.

Even for the tiniest garden this weeping effect can be obtained with some of the smaller shrubs. One useful family are the cotoneasters which if planted above a wall or rock will send down long trailing shoots which will quickly clothe the area. *Cotoneaster dammeri* is ideal for this and is studded with brilliant red berries in autumn. Another variety is *C. hybridus pendulus* with similar habit, and if grown on a stem it will make a small weeping tree. There are few shrubs that are willing to grow downwards in this way and they should not be overlooked. A third weeping cotoneaster wider than high is Merriot Weeper with evergreen leaves and red berries in small clusters, and it is a most useful shrub for uneven areas.

One of the finest specimen trees that will suit almost any situation is the Indian bean; *Catalpa bignonioides,* and although it is a tree that will not hurry and rarely shows a leaf until the end of May, its broad heart-shaped leaves and masses of flowers are well worth waiting for. In the first season after planting it is sometimes reluctant to put out leaves until late summer and one spends several months examining the stump almost daily and making apologies for it to gardening friends. Its growth during the first few years is slow but it does eventually reach magnificent proportions with large sweeping branches that will in time touch to the ground. Unless one has a garden of parkland proportions this trait should be discouraged by careful pruning. Treated this way it is a good tree for small or town gardens. It does exceptionally well in built-up areas and several fine specimens can be seen flourishing only a few yards from continual traffic. Diesel fumes and dirt seem to have little effect on it and the light green leaves always look clean and respectable.

A good specimen grown as it should be on a lawn, with ample space to spread into its natural umbrella shape, is a wonderful sight in high summer and in August the panicles of foxglove-like flowers appear, white with purple-brown spots on the inside. These develop in late September into the beans which give the tree its name. They are long and thin rather like runner beans from 8 to 15in long and decorate the tree for some time after the leaves have fallen. The one unattractive feature of this tree is the sight of dead and fallen leaves lying on the lawns or borders. Their very size stifles any growth beneath them and cannot be cleared away too soon.

The golden form of catalpa is the same in every respect except for its wonderful golden-green leaves. It is one of the finest golden deciduous trees, slow growing and far superior to the type.

167

✧✧✧✧✧✧✧✧✧✧✧

Tree of Heaven

Of that other good town tree, *Ailanthus altissima,* the Tree of Heaven, it is said that it is so called because of its noble proportions and height. Indeed, standing beneath a fine specimen one can look up and up into its towering height and gaze on successive tiers of spreading branches that seemingly reach to the heavens. Other authorities will have it that the name was given to signify the high altitudes which are supposed to be its native habitat. In deep loam the tree of heaven will thrive and grow at a rapid rate, quickly taking on its tall round-headed shape, and in maturity towering above most of its neighbours. It is well known as a tree that grows in Brooklyn, being tolerant of fog, smog and smoke, none of these conditions seeming to retard its growth.

This tall deciduous genus of about nine species is native to south-east Asia and northern Australia; while there is little obvious difference between the species, the one most generally grown and the only one usually available is *A. altissima,* sometimes listed as *A. glandulosa.*

The tree was first grown in England and France from seeds sent from China by d'Incarville, a missionary plant hunter, who collected many fine plants in the mountains near Peking in the mid-eighteenth century. It was he who first named this plant the 'stinking ash'. For a so-called heavenly tree this is a strange alias but the male flowers have an evil and offensive smell nullifying any qualities the tree might have for park planting. The male and female flowers are borne on separate trees, and this allows the latter to be planted avoiding any noticeable smell. The flowers when they do appear are not particularly striking on so large a tree, being of a greenish-yellow colour. When seed does set the result is a large terminal cluster of winged keys, the individual wings up to 2in long. These are much more decorative than the flowers and are most impressive combined with the enormous ash-like leaves of eleven to twenty-five leaflets. The ailanthus is a fast growing tree and young plants which are usually propagated from suckers can be cut back annually. If the resulting new growth is then pruned ruthlessly one has spectacular foliage shrubs of great beauty. The variety *A. pendulifolia* with large drooping leaves is well suited to this treatment and if one has the space available it could make an interesting experiment.

Conifers

In any plantation of fine and mature trees, one that can be guaranteed to be remarked on is the Ginkgo. Besides being one of the most stately and ornamental of trees it is also one of the oldest known. It is now solely represented by the one surviving form, *Ginkgo biloba*, from a family of trees that grew over a wide area many millions of years ago. In the East its age has given it religious significance and as a sacred tree it is often found in the vicinity of Buddhist monasteries.

The characteristic shape of a mature specimen of this deciduous conifer depends to a certain extent on choosing the correct site for planting. While the tree is perfectly hardy it does prefer some shelter from wind to allow its branches to assume their natural wand-like position. Young plants show little promise of the grace of the older trees and can on occasion be rather gawky. Ginkgos appreciate a good soil and growing conditions and except on favourable sites can be erratic in growth in the early years, but once established the rate increases more evenly. On good deep dry loam a 30ft specimen can be expected in twenty-five years. Flowers and fruit are insignificant but the strange fan-shaped leaves are beautiful in all their stages and reliably turn to a clear butter yellow in the autumn before falling.

Most conifers contribute to the autumn scene by the contrast their deep green needles provide to the brighter tints of the broad-leaved trees. The deciduous conifers have their own special quality of autumn colour from the clear butter yellow of the Ginkgo and the mellow ochre of the larch to the shining bronze of the swamp cypress. The latter, *Taxodium distichum,* a native of North and Central America, is exceptionally beautiful in all seasons of the year and its brief period of autumn colour is one to be anticipated. There are few finer sights than a mature specimen towering above the water's edge reflecting its foxy red foliage in still water on a clear autumn day.

For wet soils and planting directly at the water's edge, there is no better tree. They will thrive in water-logged soils where few others would survive, although it is essential that the initial planting be made on a slight mound in these situations. Eventually the trunk becomes strongly proportioned, with stout jutting buttresses, at the base. The fibrous bark is an attractive russet red. A remarkable feature of mature specimens are the protruding growths known as 'knees' which arise a foot or so from old roots. These hollow projections which stand above soil and water presumably assist the plant's respiratory system.

The foliage in the growing season is remarkably beautiful and stands out from its neighbours by its brilliance and boldness. Strong fronds of yellow-green leaves swirl spirally around persistant branchlets that bear male and female flowers. In winter long purple catkins decorate the branches of mature specimens.

8

Evergreens

There are those who can only tolerate the winter months as a time of anticipation of better things to come; although others find much to enjoy in winter foliage and flowers. Most of the plants that we regard as winter flowering do not come into bloom until the new year and from November onwards decorative evergreen foliage begins to earn its keep.

With the wealth of plant material available today, planning for colour in the winter garden is hardly less difficult than furnishing a full summer border. Long periods of colour can be arranged with evergreen and variegated foliage.

Hollies

All evergreens are useful for clothing the garden in winter and those that have bold variegation help to add colour to the general scene. Hollies are the toughest of evergreens always having an appearance of robust good health and are rarely affected by the worst wind or cold. One of the finest sights of winter is a well-grown variegated form lit by a wintery sun; in a season when berries are abundant the picture is complete.

The aquifolium section of hollies are tolerant of all conditions and soils and there are a dozen or more varieties available with striking variegated foliage in silver and gold. Among these Madame Briot is one of the best garden plants with plentiful berries that crop regularly and show up well against conspicuous leaves edged with gold. For cooler schemes *Ilex myrtifolia variegata* has an edging of palest cream and combines well with the light yellows and blues of early spring bulbs.

With the vast amount of folklore that has accumulated around most familiar plants over the centuries it is not surprising that the holly and the ivy, two very common evergreens, have been held in continual esteem. Both plants can always be relied on to give cheerful evergreen leaves in the dead of winter, and in a good season the holly can be covered in scarlet berries. Legends associated with the holly in particular vary according to the beliefs and sophistication of the times. The derivation of the religious symbolism is not difficult to imagine. The purity of the white flowers which open in May, the blood-red berries and the prickly leaves representing the crown of thorns were powerful symbols.

Of all the material available for winter decoration these two were the most powerful living emblems and always there for the gathering. In a more superstitious age holly would be planted near the house to deter witches, and in many parts of the country there was a belief that trimming or cutting holly, even if it formed part of a hedge, would bring bad luck. The practise of hanging branches of holly and ivy in the house from Christmas Eve to Candlemas Eve was supposed to subdue the house goblins and the decorative aspect was originally of little importance.

Although there are several excellent garden cultivars of holly available, only the common *Ilex aquifolium* looks right in the rural setting and is well worth a place in the modern garden if space permits. When allowed to grow freely the holly makes a fine single trunked tree with a tapering head, its lower branches only being set with spiked leaves. As a hedging plant it has no equal for good looks, and it makes a thick impenetrable barrier. Only its slow rate of growth prevents it from being used more widely for this purpose.

Unfortunately this plant is more often seen as a straggly bush forming part of the undergrowth of much of our deciduous woodlands. The berries which appear on the female trees are favourite food for many birds, although inexplicably they can be choosy and strip a plant bare at one time and ignore it at another.

There are many good garden forms of *I. aquifolium*; all of them hardy and differing in shape and colour. The variegated forms are splendid plants for the winter garden and for best effect should be planted where the sun will strike them. A delightful weeping variegated form known as Perry's Silver can be relied on for an annual crop of berries. For the ultimate in prickly leaves there is the hedgehog holly, *I. aquifolium ferox*, with spines on the upper surface of the leaves as well as the edges. This variety has both golden and silver variegated forms.

Ivy

Anyone can grow ivies and more gardeners should experiment with the wide range of these hardy plants that will thrive in almost any soil and situation. It is only in recent years that outdoor ivies have begun to regain favour as useful and valuable garden material flourishing where few other plants would survive. Many gardeners shy away at the mention of ivy believing that either it is too rampant in borders or insidious and harmful when grown on walls. With the large-leaved ivies the first charge is certainly true, but for ground cover under trees and masking large unsightly areas this is a decided asset. There are two schools of thought about ivy on walls. Some will not tolerate it at any price for its waywardness in creeping under tiles and between crevices in brickwork. All clinging plants need to be kept within bounds and away from roof tiles, but will do no harm to sound mortar joints between bricks. Indeed lovers of ivy-clad walls will hold forth the theory that the leaves actually protect the brickwork against harmful chemical fumes abounding in the atmosphere of a highly industrialised country. But for those who do not wish to give up good garden space or risk damaging walls, there are always situations in most gardens where little else will grow except ivies. One of the commoner practices is to cover old tree stumps that are too large to remove. These are ideal hosts for an evergreen covering and *Hedera hibernica,* the Irish ivy with large angular leaves, will give rapid cover. This ivy takes on purple tones in the winter and will grow in the most unpromising places.

Another large leaved ivy is *H. colchica dentata.* Its variegated form is of superb colouring with pale yellow, grey and green patterning each leaf. These in mass on wall, fence or balustrade make one of the most striking evergreen screens. Some of the smaller variegated ivies are far less rampant and can be controlled with ease. One way of growing these is along the risers of garden steps where they will cling quite happily and soften the harsh lines of stonework. Providing stray shoots are cut off each year and the overhang of the step is sufficient there is no danger of catching one's foot in the growth as might be supposed.

Smaller ivies can be trained and controlled for many purposes besides use on vertical walls or under trees.

It is not so many years ago that the now popular *Hedera helix,* Gold Heart, was not so easy to come by and gardeners who were lucky enough to possess it worried unduly over its hardiness as an outdoor plant. It has however proved to be capable of standing against the worst of conditions and will thrive happily on a north wall.

The silver variegation of the medium-sized *Hedera helix* Glacier gives a most satisfactory effect at any time of the year and will obligingly climb and embellish stonework or grow horizontally to give good ground cover with equal ease. At the base of some dark conifer, it will do much to brighten an otherwise dead planting in the winter when there are few flowers to relieve the gloom. By careful initial training and subsequent clipping or pinching out it can be persuaded to follow almost any contour and highly decorative effects can be produced by even the most ham-handed gardener.

The small leaved ivy Green Ripple has sharply pointed leaves growing in such profusion that it quickly makes a solid sculptured mass. It is an extremely attractive variety and one of the best for training into a ribbon of green and used as an edging or a cap to a low retaining wall.

Probably the greatest virtue of the ivy family is its ability to thrive in places where nothing else will survive. In dense shade below trees and shrubs, it will make splendid cover over what would otherwise be an area of damp rank ground unfavourable even to weeds and grass. As town plants for difficult and sunless corners they are no less adaptable and their complete immunity to atmospheric pollution enables them to be used with confidence near industrial sites.

Arboreal forms provide us with long lasting winter decoration in the form of geometrically-shaped flowers and shining blue berries: these neglected shrubby forms are beginning to receive the recognition they deserve as plants that can help to give sense of maturity and form in the winter garden. The strange flowers which begin to bloom in October are attractive to bees and wasps and can be covered with these on a fine day in late autumn. For the best show of flowers and berries the plain green varieties with dark shining leaves produce their own perfect background.

Tree forms of the larger-leaved variegated species also have similar flowers but the effect is not so good and becomes somewhat confused.

Euonymus

Of the smaller evergreens that can give colour in the winter border there are none better than the variegated forms of euonymus with silver or gold variegations to the leaves.

The best known and probably the most useful is *E. fortunei*, Silver Queen, whose qualities lie in its dwarf and slow growing habit and willingness to put up with most situations providing it is given a fairly sheltered position. As an edging plant where it can gradually creep over adjacent stonework its brilliant green and silver leaves show to advantage and soften the hardest lines. On the coldest days, this plant takes on attractive pink tints in its variegated parts and rarely looks dejected as do some evergreens. Grown at the foot of a wall this plant will demonstrate its climbing capabilities by slowly covering the wall with arching branches. Although slow growing this is one of the easiest evergreens to propagate by layering and pegging the lower branches into good soil conditioned with sand and peat.

The various forms of *Euonymus japonica* are ideal shrubs for coastal planting and are large enough to make presentable hedges. In this species there is a greater choice of variegated cultivars with large or small leaves and variegated centres or edgings in silver or gold.

Mass plantings of these shrubs usually achieves only a spotty effect but individual plants strategically placed to lighten stretches of more sober green has greater import. As specimen bushes set against a wall where they will receive some protection they can be relied on to brighten the winter garden.

The evergreen varieties of the eleagnus family are invaluable shrubs being of modest size and fairly slow growth. The most handsome of these is *E. pungens aureo variegata* with two-toned green leaves that are splashed with gold. The undersides of these leaves are rough and have a mineral quality rather like glass paper. The same quality is apparent in the young leaves which are completely covered with dull golden scales. When the old leaves do die off, usually as the new ones appear, they take on a wonderful cadmium orange tone which is quite unique among garden plants. The other valuable shrub belonging to the family is *E. pungens dicksonii* and here the pattern of the leaf is reversed. The golden foliage has a central green stripe and this form is best grown in shade. There is nothing quite like these shrubs for brightening a dark corner. They are at their best in winter for the colder the day the brighter the leaves seem to shine and add brilliance of colour at a time of the year when little else is available.

Juniper

The ideal ground cover which never varies and does its work suppressing weeds and keeping the ground respectably clothed throughout the year must be evergreen and forceful enough to cover the ground at a reasonable rate. Some evergreens are anything but reasonable in their rate of growth and romp away, needing constant attention to keep them within bounds. Of the low growing shrubby evergreens, some of the conifers are just right for this work and none better than the prostrate junipers, since they will grow in almost any situation and are not at all fussy about soil. Like all junipers they will thrive in chalk, and will also grow quite happily in clay or neutral soil. This family has about a dozen good prostrate and creeping varieties that will make good ground cover and are useful for covering banks and awkward corners.

Few things are more suited to covering uneven ground than *Juniperus sabina tamariscifolia,* one of the most attractive of all with its flattened branches. This Spanish juniper is extremely vigorous and will cover a fair sized area in a short time. *Juniperus horizontalis* will also cover wide expanses and this variety has both blue-leaved and variegated forms. Another good variety but with a little more height is *J. chinensis japonica,* more slow in growth but with the same spreading habit. It will take a dozen years or more to reach 2ft.

One of the most decorative varieties, particularly in its variegated form is *Juniperus expansa.* The foliage here is flecked prominently with yellow at the tips of the fan like branches.

The common juniper, a native of our chalk downs, contributes with *Juniper communis prostrata* a valuable creeping form that rarely raises its head more than a foot and like all the natives is extremely hardy. The mat forming species from maritime districts of Japan known as the Shore Juniper, *J. conferta,* looks well on a rockery where it will throw out long arms clothed with the typical needle-like foliage. From the mountains of the same country, *J. procumbens* rises only an inch or so above the ground and is a very tough and rugged plant. As can be seen, there is a good variety of foliage colour and shape in these plants together with the attraction of the juvenile leaves which are quite different from the adult scales. The typical odour associated with these junipers is another asset which makes them worth considering for any slope.

Index

179

Index

Index